30-Day Hearty Vegan Keto Meal Plan & Recipes

Over 100 Delicious Vegan Ketogenic Recipes For Healthy Living

AMY ZACKARY

ISBN-13:978-1986493673

ISBN-10:1986493679

DEDICATION

For Cindy,

Pleasant memories, always!

TABLE OF CONTENTS

Other Books By Amy Zackary

The Anti-Inflammation Cookbook: Scrumptious Recipes To Fight Inflammatory Diseases & Restore Overall Health

Fatty Liver: Recipes And Guide To Prevent And Reverse Fatty Liver, Lose Weight And Live Longer

INTRODUCTION

Vegan Ketogenic Dieting And Meal Planning

Meal planning is crucial to dieting, especially a ketogenic diet. The ketogenic diet is an ultra-low carbohydrate and high fat diet. This type of diet is different from other low carb eating as it aims to change the body's main source of energy to ketosis. The ketogenic diet, or keto diet, has been proven to be very effective against many chronic illnesses and diseases that people regularly struggle with. For instance, it helps to reverse diabetes, alleviate epilepsy, battle cancer, counter obesity, lower blood pressure and prevent neurodegenerative diseases such as Parkinson's disease and Alzheimer's disease.

Unfortunately, a vegan diet, which is high carb, cannot help much with any of these diseases. So while vegans are concerned about alleviating animal suffering by non-consumption of animal products, which are generally high in fats, they may miss out on the tremendous health benefits of the ketogenic diet since they cannot get their fats from animal-based products …unless, they find a way to tweak these two eating styles to suit them. This is possible. Therefore, a vegan ketogenic diet is a combination of the vegan diet and the keto diet with the ultimate goal of achieving ketosis and enjoying optimal health.

The macronutrient ratios of the ketogenic diet are about 70 to 80% fat, 15 to 25% protein and 5% carbohydrates. This macronutrient ratio is non-negotiable. Also non-negotiable as vegans, is the non-consumption of animal products, such as meat and dairy. However, the information below will help to shed more light on macronutrients and their sources for the vegan ketogenic diet:

Carbs

You only need a total caloric intake of 5% or less of carbohydrate. This should be 30-35 net grams, excluding fiber. Regular ketogenic dieters can even do less than that and get to ketosis faster. Since all plant- based foods contain carbs, vegan ketogenic dieters, however, will have to strive to maintain this amount of carb intake, especially at the adaptation phase. But, after achieving ketosis for the first time, the amount of carb intake may be increased from 35grams to about 50 grams, but no more.

Get rid of all carbs that contain white flour and refined sugar. Get rid of all heavily processed carbs and look for carbs that are high in fiber. Your Sources of low carb should include: Lettuce, beet greens, kale, bokchoy, spinach, cucumber, Swiss chard, alfalfa sprouts, Swiss chard, cauliflower, celery, tomatoes, lettuce, eggplant, and asparagus. Also included are berries such as rhubarb, raspberries, blueberries, strawberries and blackberries

Fats

Stay away from refined vegetable oils and transfats, such as canola oil, rapeseed oil and margarine. Fat sources for the vegan ketogenic should include: Avocado oils, cocoa butter, coconut oil, flaxseed oil, macadamia oil, MCT oil, olive oil, red palm oil, coconut cream, olives, avocados and coconut milk

Protein

Thankfully, you don't need too much protein. You only need 0.7 to 1 grams per pound of lean body weight. If you're sedentary, you need less.

Sources of protein include firm tofu, hard nigari tofu, pumpkin seeds, extra firm silken tofu, almonds, soft silken tofu, flaxseed, chia seeds, Brazil nuts and hazelnuts.

To implement the vegan keto diet correctly:

1. Of course you'll have to do away with all meat, fish and seafood as well as other animal products from your diet but remember your:

- Total carbohydrate consumption should be 35 grams or less per day.
- 70% of your calories must come from plant-based fats.
- About 25% of your calories must come from plant-based proteins.

2. Take Supplements to help with nutrients such as iron and vitamins D3, B12 and B6.

3. Eat lots of low-carb veggies.

4. Ensure they are no hidden carbs, added sugar or hydrogenated oils in the keto-friendly vegan dairy products that you buy.

5. Avoid meat substitutes.

6. Eat soy sparingly because it contains certain plant compounds that can damage thyroid function.

7. PLAN YOUR MEALS.

As restrictive as the vegan ketogenic diet is, it can still be tweaked to provide the needed health benefits. This is why meal planning is important.

Meal Planning will:

- Enable you attain ketosis faster by making healthier choices.
- Add variety to your meals.
- Ensure you eat high quality vegan ketogenic foods
- Help you save money and time
- Reduce the stress of thinking about what to buy and eat, how to tweak food or substitute one non-vegan ingredient with a vegan one.

- Help to avoid buying the wrong ingredients.
- Prepare you for future meals.

Your Everyday Vegan Keto Pantry

Having certain ingredients within reach makes it easier to be versatile with your cooking, as well as plan and prepare delicious vegan ketogenic meals anytime of the day. Some of these ingredients needed in your pantry are:

Avocados: avocados are one of the best forms of healthy fat. It can be used as base for salad dressings and sauces. It is also very filling as a snack with just a little sprinkling of pepper and salt.

Chia Seeds: Chia seeds can absorb liquid and multiply in size. It can be used as an appetite suppressant and as a "pudding" or spread using almond milk or any other a non-dairy milk. It easily modified with sweeteners and cinnamon or even raspberries.

Flax Seed: low in carbs but high in healthy fats, flax seed is your ideal ingredient that can be used for virtually anything. Since it binds food easily, it is a great substitute for egg, especially in vegan baking.

Hemp Hearts: very tiny, nutty in taste and texture, Hemp Hearts are loaded with fiber and fats. Besides its ketogenic benefits, it aids digestion and mental clarity. They are also easy to add to meals. Simply sprinkle them over a smoothie bowl, mix into fried veggies or top on a salad.

Cauliflower: mild in taste and texture, cauliflower makes a great substitute for carb-rich foods like potatoes. It can be enjoyed raw, steamed, mashed or roasted. It is used in making the very popular cauliflower rice. See recipe below.

Full Fat Coconut Milk: Get all the healthy fats that you need with Full Fat Coconut Milk. It can also serve as a perfect base for your veggie tofu curry, your creamy broccoli soup, or that spicy creamed spinach.

Raspberries: Antioxidants- rich raspberries are one of the very few fruits that make it to the list of vegan keto diet. Why? It is low in net carbs, so you can satisfy your sweet tooth and still maintain ketosis.

Vegan Protein Powders: ketogenic compliant, vegan protein powders are readily available, so this shouldn't pose a problem when you want to buy. They will help boost your protein and sustain you all through the day. However, while mixing dairy free milk, see to it that it is natural sugar-free milk like almond milk.

Broccoli: low-carb, low fat broccoli is a superb addition to your meal options. It is very healthy as the protein in one serving bowl can be compared to a serving of beef per100 calories. It can be enjoyed with coconut curries, vegan stir-fries with loads of good coconut oils or any other healthy fats.

Mushrooms: Mushrooms are versatile. They can be grilled, roasted, stuffed or made into a soup. They are a mild flavor but emerge very flavorful as they cook.

Coconut Butter: Coconut butter is actually coconut flesh that's pureed into a spread. It comes in solid in a jar, but when melted a bit and mixed well, the resulting taste is like frosting.

90-99% Dark Chocolate: Dark chocolates are very beneficial. They help to lower blood pressure, improve the skin and fight depression. Antioxidant-rich dark chocolates must have a very high percentage for it to be effective for vegan keto dieters. The higher the percentage, the lower the sugar and carbs.

Zucchini: cut zucchini with a spiralizer and enjoy the wonderful ways to make it pasta-like. It can be sliced thin, oiled lightly, seasoned and roasted. You can also make it into chips and enjoy as snacks. Chill it and see how it works as a base for a cold salad.

Vegan Mayonnaise: while it contains no protein, it's high in fat. It can be used as an excellent base for salad dressings and spreads.

Other vegan ingredients that make for great ketogenic cooking include cashew cheese, spaghetti squash, tofu, Shiraki Noodles, pecans and hot sauce

A 30-Day Vegan Ketogenic Meal Plan

All meal plans include nutritional information for calories, fat, net carbs and protein.

DAY 1

BREAKFAST

Chia Chocolate Pudding

Enjoy a nourishing breakfast that'll keep you full and energetic for the better part of the day.

Servings: 1

Preparation time: 5 minutes

Cooking time: 0 minutes

Ingredients:

1/2 cup of almond milk or water

1/4 cup of coconut milk

1/4 cup of whole or ground chia seeds

5-10 drops of stevia extract

1 tablespoon of powdered swerve or erythriol

1 tablespoon of unsweetened raw cocoa powder

1/2 tablespoon of raw cocoa nibs

Directions:

1. Combine all the ingredients except the cocoa nibs together. Leave to stand for 10-15 minutes at least or preferably overnight.

2. Top with the cocoa nibs and serve.

Nutrition Per Serving

Calories: 329, Fat: 25.6g, Carbohydrates: 6.3g, Protein: 9.5g

LUNCH

Cauliflower Rice

A "grain" that is low carb and incredibly nutritious.

Servings: 6

Preparation time: 5 minutes

Cooking time: 10 minutes

Ingredients:

1/2 cauliflower, remove leaves,

1 cup of full fat coconut cream

1 teaspoon of cilantro

1/4 cup of unsweetened coconut, shredded

Salt

Directions:

1. Remove the leaves of the cauliflower, its hard core centre, cut into small florets and shred in a processor.

2. Put the shredded cauliflower and the other ingredients in a large pan.

3. Cook over medium high heat until it softens.

Nutrition Per Serving

Calories: 84, Fat: 6.9g, Carbohydrates: 4.5g, Protein: 2g

DINNER

Spinach Tabbouleh

The cauliflower rice acts as a substitute for the traditional grains.

Servings: 3-4

Preparation time: 15 minutes

Cooking time: 5 minutes

Ingredients:

3 cups of cauliflower rice

3 cups of spinach, chopped

1 cup of regular or cherry tomatoes, chopped

1 cup of fresh parsley, chopped

1/2 cup of fresh lemon juice

1/2 cup of fresh mint, chopped

1/2 cup of extra virgin olive oil

2 tablespoons of extra virgin coconut oil

2 medium spring onions, chopped

1 medium cucumber, peeled and chopped

1 garlic clove, crushed

1 teaspoon of salt

1/4 teaspoon of freshly ground black pepper

Directions:

1. Heat oil in a pan over medium heat.

2. Cook the cauliflower and a pinch of salt for about 5 minutes or until it is tender and crispy while stirring occasionally. Remove from heat, keep aside to cool.

3. Add the vegetables and cooked cauliflower to a salad bowl. Mix well.

4. Whisk the garlic, lemon juice and olive oil in a bowl. Pour this mixture over the tabbouleh.

5. Add seasoning and toss with tongs or two forks to combine.

Nutrition Per Serving

Calories: 245, Fat: 23.5g, Carbohydrates: 5.4g, Protein: 2.6g

DAY 2

BREAKFAST

Protein-Rich Breakfast
Servings: 2

Preparation time: minutes

Cooking time: 5 minutes

Ingredients:

7 oz (1/2 pack) firm/extra firm tofu

1 scoop of vegan protein powder

1 cup coconut milk, un-sweetened

2 tbsp hemp hearts

1/2 oz almonds

1 tbsp cacao nibs

1 tbsp cocoa powder

1 tbsp chia seeds

15 drops liquid stevia

Directions:

1. Add together all ingredients and blend until a thick consistency is achieved.

2. Store and refrigerate for up to a week. *Enjoy!*

Nutrition Per Serving

Calories: 3.37, Fat: 20.5g, Carbohydrates: 12.5g, Protein: 28g

LUNCH

Hearty Lunch Bagels
Enjoy these little dense and hearty bagels for lunch.

Servings: 4

Preparation time: 10 minutes

Cooking time: 45minutes

Ingredients:

3 tbsp flax seeds, ground

1/4 cup psyllium powder

1/2 cup tahini

1 tsp baking powder

1/4 cup almond flour

Pinch salt, optional

1 cup water

Directions:

1. Add the ground flax seeds to the psyllium, baking powder and almond flour. Add salt, if using.

2. Combine water and tahini and mix until smooth. Add mixture to the dry mix and mix again until a dough ball is formed.

3. Break into pieces of four and make into bun shapes.

4. Bake for 45 minutes at 375°F.

5. To serve, cut in half and toast again.

Nutrition Per Serving

Calories: 292.6, Fat: 22g, Carbohydrates: 6.1g, Protein: 8.6g

DINNER

Red Gazpacho
Enjoy this light Spanish delicacy for dinner.

Servings: 6

Preparation time: 20 minutes

Cooking time: 20 minutes

Ingredients:

1 cup of extra virgin olive oil

2-4 tablespoons of chopped fresh parsley

2-4 tablespoons of chopped fresh basil

2 tablespoons of wine or apple cider vinegar

2 tablespoons of fresh lemon juice

4-5 medium tomatoes, quartered

2 medium spring onions, sliced

2 garlic cloves, peeled

2 medium avocados, peeled, halved and seeded

1 large cucumber, diced

1 large red pepper, halved, cored and seeded

1 large green pepper, halved, cored and seeded

1 small red onion, peeled and roughly chopped

14

1 teaspoon of salt

Freshly ground black pepper

Directions:

1. Preheat oven to 400°F and line a baking pan with parchment paper.

2. Place the green and red peppers on the baking pan with its cut side facing down and roast in the oven for about 20 minutes or until it begins to blacken and its skin blisters. Remove and keep aside to cool. Peel the skin and discard.

3. Process the red onion, tomatoes, avocados, roasted peppers, parsley, basil, lemon juice, olive oil, garlic, vinegar, salt and pepper in a blender until smooth.

4. Add the spring onions and cucumber; mix with the soup to combine.

5. Adjust seasoning if desired.

Nutrition Per Serving

Calories: 528, Fat: 50.8g, Carbohydrates: 8.5g, Protein: 7.5g

DAY 3

BREAKFAST

Green Chocolate Smoothie
It is healthy and delicious.

Servings: 2

Preparation time: 5 minutes

Cooking time: 0 minutes

Ingredients:

3 1/2 ounces of chopped spinach

1 cup of coconut cream

1/2 cup of frozen berries

1/4 cup of cocoa powder

1 tablespoon of granulated sugar substitute

Directions:

Blend all the ingredients together until smooth.

Nutrition Per Serving

Calories: 362, Fat: 33.5g, Carbohydrates: 7.6g, Protein: 7.5g

LUNCH

Zoodles Radicchio Salad
A vegan delight made with walnuts and parmesan.

Servings: 4

Preparation time: 15 minutes

Cooking time: 0 minutes

Ingredients:

Dressing:

1/3 cup of avocado oil

1/4 cup of lemon juice, freshly squeezed

1 teaspoon of fresh garlic, crushed

1/2 teaspoon of granulated sugar substitute

Pepper

Kosher salt

Salad:

4 cups of zucchini, spiralized

1 cup of fresh radicchio, shredded

1 ounce of shaved vegan Parmesan cheese

1/4 cup of coarsely chopped walnuts

1/4 cup of coarsely chopped parsley

Directions:

1. Whisk the dressing ingredients in a small bowl.

2. In a medium bowl, gently mix the salad ingredients together.

3. Drizzle the dressing over the salad and toss to coat.

Nutrition Per Serving

Calories: 265, Fat: 25g, Carbohydrates: 5.5g, Protein: 6g

DINNER

Chipotle Pumpkin Soup
A pleasantly-tasting soup you'd love!

Servings: 6

Preparation time: 5 minutes

Cooking time: 16 minutes

Ingredients:

32 ounces of vegetable broth

2 cups of pumpkin purée

1/2 cup of coconut cream

1/2 cup of chopped onions

2 tablespoons of olive oil

1 tablespoon of chipotles in adobo sauce

1 garlic clove, chopped

2 teaspoons of granulated sugar substitute

2 teaspoons of red wine vinegar

1 teaspoon of ground cumin

1 teaspoon of ground coriander

1/8 teaspoon of ground allspice

Salt

Pepper

Directions:

1. In a medium pan, heat oil and sauté the garlic and onions for 3-4 minutes until translucent.

2. Add the cumin, chipotles, sugar substitute, coriander and allspice; cook for an additional 2 minutes.

3. Add the broth and puree; let it simmer for about 5 minutes.

4. Transfer the soup to a blender and blend until smooth.

5. Return soup to pot, add the vinegar and cream; give it time to simmer for 5 minutes.

6. Season with salt and pepper.

Nutrition Per Serving

Calories: 138, Fat: 12g, Carbohydrates: 6g, Protein: 2g

DAY 4

BREAKFAST

Overnight Vanilla Oats
An easy breakfast that's also lifesaving!

Servings: 2

Preparation time: 15 minutes

Cooking time: 0 minutes

Ingredients:

1/2 cup of hemp hearts

2/3 cup of full fat coconut milk

1 tablespoon of chia seeds

2 teaspoons of erythriol

A pinch of Himalayan rock salt, finely ground

1/2 teaspoon of vanilla extract

Directions:

1. Combine all the ingredients together in a bowl.

2. Cover and refrigerate for at least 8 hours or overnight.

3. Stir in extra milk the next day and serve.

Nutrition Per Serving

Calories: 408, Fat: 34.7g, Carbohydrates: 9.1g, Protein: 15.3g

LUNCH

Caesar Salad

Servings: 4

Preparation time: 5 minutes

Cooking time: 0 minutes

Ingredients:

12 cups of romaine leaves, chopped

1/4 cup of hemp seeds

1 ripe avocado

3 garlic cloves, crushed

3 tablespoons of lemon juice

2 tablespoons of water

1 tablespoon of capers

1 tablespoon of caper brine

2 teaspoons of Dijon mustard

Sea salt

Freshly ground pepper

Directions:

1. Blend all the ingredients except the hemp seeds and romaine in a blender or food processor until smooth.

2. Pour into a bowl, add the hemp seeds and stir.

3. In a large bowl, place the romaine leaves, add the blended mixture and combine with the leaves to coat.

Nutrition Per Serving

Calories: 168, Fat: 12.5g, Carbohydrates: 5.2g, Protein: 6.6g

DINNER

Thyme And Cauliflower Soup
It is warm, comforting and satisfying.

Servings: 6

Preparation time: 10 minutes

Cooking time: 20 minutes

Ingredients:

1 head of cauliflower, chopped into florets

3 cups of vegetable broth

5 cloves of garlic, chopped

1 tablespoon of olive oil

2 teaspoon of thyme powder

1 teaspoon of ground black pepper

1 teaspoon of Celtic sea salt

1/2 teaspoon of match green tea powder

Directions:

1. Heat the broth, mix the powder and thyme in a large pot over medium high heat; let it come to a boil.

2. Add the cauliflower and cook for about 10 minutes until it is soft.

3. Meanwhile, heat oil in a small pan and sauté the garlic for about 1 minute until fragrant.

4. Add the sautéed garlic, salt and pepper to the pot when the cauliflower becomes soft. Cook for an additional 1-2 minutes.

6. Remove from heat, transfer to an immersion blender and blend until smooth.

Nutrition Per Serving

Calories: 51, Fat: 2.4g, Carbohydrates: 6.7g, Protein: 1.5g

DAY 5

Flaxseed Waffles
It contains no flour and comes out crispy.

Servings: 4

Preparation time: 10 minutes

Cooking time: 25 minutes

Ingredients:

2 cups of golden flaxseed, coarsely ground

1/2 cup of water

1/3 cup of melted coconut oil

5 tablespoons of finely ground flaxseed mixed with 15 tablespoons of warm water

1 tablespoon of baking powder

2 teaspoons of ground cinnamon

1 teaspoon of sea salt

Directions:

1. Preheat the waffle iron over medium heat.

2. In a large bowl, mix the baking powder, flaxseed and salt together. Set aside.

3. Blend the water, finely ground flaxseed mixture and coconut oil in a blender until it foams.

4. Pour this mixture into the baking powder mixture and combine thoroughly with a spatula until it becomes fluffy. Leave to stand for 3 minutes.

5. Stir in the cinnamon and evenly divide the batter into 4 portions.

6. Cook the batter one at a time.

Nutrition Per Serving

Calories: 550, Fat: 42g, Carbohydrates: 3g, Protein: 18.3g

LUNCH

Greek Cucumber Salad
A delicious Mediterranean fare.

Servings: 6

Preparation time: 10 minutes

Cooking time: 0 minutes

Ingredients:

1 1/2 ounces of red onion, coarsely chopped

1/2 cup of kalamata olives

1/2 cup of raw cashew

1/2 cup of sun-dried tomatoes

1 avocado, peeled, pit removed and cut into cubes

2 large cucumbers, cut into half lengthwise and sliced

Directions:

Combine all the ingredients in a large bowl and toss with dressing.

Calories: 246, Fat: 17.5g, Carbohydrates: 9g, Protein: 9.5g

DINNER

Asparagus Hazelnut Soup
A great cold reliever.

Servings: 4

Preparation time: 20 minutes

Cooking time: 15 minutes

Ingredients:

2 1/2 cups of fresh asparagus, cut and trimmed

2 cups of vegetable stock

1/2 cup of unsweetened almond milk

1/2 cup of sweet onion, chopped

1/3 cup of toasted whole hazelnuts

3 cloves of garlic, diced

2 tablespoons of lemon juice

2 tablespoons of fresh basil, chopped

1 tablespoon of olive oil

2 teaspoons of low sodium soy sauce

1/4 teaspoon of salt

A dash of crushed red pepper flakes

Shaved asparagus, optional

Directions:

1. Heat the olive oil in a large pan over medium heat and sauté the garlic, pepper flakes and onion for 4-5 minutes until the onion is tender.

2. Add the stock and asparagus; leave to boil.

3. Lower the heat, simmer for 6-8 minutes while covered until the asparagus is soft. Remove pan from heat and let it cool a bit.

4. Blend the basil, lemon juice and hazelnuts in a blender.

5. Add the cooked asparagus to the blender and purée until it is creamy and smooth.

6. Return the pureed mixture to the pan and add the milk, salt and soy sauce.

7. Stir the soup but do not allow it boil.

8. Garnish with the shaved asparagus and serve.

Nutrition Per Serving

Calories: 164, Fat: 13g, Carbohydrates: 7g, Protein: 5g

DAY 6

BREAKFAST

Pistachio Avocado Toast
A filling breakfast.

Servings: 1

Preparation time: 5 minutes

Cooking time: 0 minutes

Ingredients:

6 pistachios, minced

1 slice of toasted vegan keto crisp bread (see below) or any other vegan keto bread

1/8 tomato, chopped

1/2 ripe avocado, cut in half

2 teaspoons of extra virgin olive oil

1/2 teaspoon of lime juice

Sea salt

Directions:

1. Drizzle the lime juice over the cut avocado.

2. Set the avocado on the bread and mash it into the bread.

3. Sprinkle the pistachios, tomatoes and salt over the toast.

4. Drizzle the oil over it and serve.

Nutrition Per Serving

Calories: 376, Fat: 38g, Carbohydrates: 3g, Protein: 5g

To Make Vegan Keto Crisp Bread

Takes time to cook, but it's worth it at the end of the day!

Servings: 20 crisp bread

Preparation time: 30 minutes

Cooking time: 1 hour, 45 minutes

Ingredients:

1 cup raw sunflower seeds

1 cup sesame seeds

1 cup flax seed

3 tbsp psyllium husk

½ cup hemp seed, hulled

1 teaspoon salt

2 cups water

1 tsp baking powder

Directions:

1. Preheat oven to 350°F. Pulverize the seeds, baking powder, pysllium husk and salt in a food processor until sand-like.

2. Add the water and mix until uniformed batter is formed. Let it rest 10 minutes to thicken and look more like dough.

3. Spread dough in lined cookie sheet and bake for an hour and 15 minutes or when everything, including the centre is firm.

4. Cut into 20 pieces and let it cook for 30 minutes. *Enjoy!* (Bread loses its crispness after 5 days. Therefore, reheat in the oven or toaster before eating)

Nutrition Per Serving

Calories: 156, Fat: 13.2g, Carbohydrates: 1g, Protein: 5.5g

LUNCH

Asian Slaw
An attractive and enticing lunch idea.

Servings: 6

Preparation time: 15 minutes

Cooking time: 0 minutes

Ingredients:

1 cup of snow peas, sliced into thin sticks

1/4 cup of rice wine vinegar

4 whole scallions

4 cloves of garlic, crushed

2 small red bell peppers, seeded and thinly sliced

1 small head of Napa cabbage, shredded

1 large carrot, peeled and sliced into thin sticks

1 medium red onion, thinly sliced

2 tablespoons low carb sweetener of choice

2 tablespoons of sesame oil

2 tablespoons of black sesame seeds

1 tablespoon of chopped fresh ginger

Salt

Pepper

Directions:

1. Combine all the ingredients in a large bowl.

2. Allow to stand for about 10 minutes.

3. Toss again and serve.

Nutrition Per Serving

Calories: 132.41, Fat: 6.59g, Carbohydrates: 7.9g, Protein: 2.95g

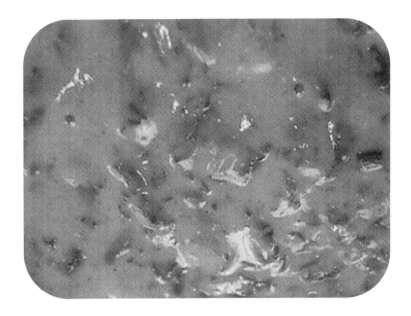

DINNER

Creamy Green Soup

A healthy bowl of nourishing goodness.

Servings: 4

Preparation time: 5 minutes

Cooking time: 0 minutes

Ingredients:

2 cups of spinach leaves

1/4 cup of vegetable stock

1/2 cup of English cucumbers

1/2 cup of red bell peppers

1 garlic clove

1 avocado

1 green onion

1 tablespoon of lemon juice

1 tablespoon of soy seasoning

Freshly ground pepper

A pinch of chili powder, optional

Directions:

Blend all the ingredients together in a blender until smooth and creamy.

Nutrition Per Serving

Calories: 95, Fat: 7.6g, Carbohydrates: 6.7g, Protein: 2.1g

DAY 7

BREAKFAST

Vegan Pancakes

Add your favorite toppings for a delicious breakfast.

Servings: 1

Preparation time: 10 minutes

Cooking time: 7 minutes

Ingredients:

2 tablespoons of vanilla vegan powder

1 1/2 tablespoons of coconut oil

1 tablespoons of ground flaxseed mixed with 3 tablespoons of water

1 tablespoon of flaxseed, ground

1/4 teaspoon of baking powder

A pinch of salt

Directions:

1. Combine the dry ingredients in a bowl.

2. In another bowl, combine the wet ingredients together.

3. Add the wet ingredients to the dry ingredients and combine thoroughly.

4. Grease a pan lightly and heat over medium heat.

5. Evenly divide the batter into 3 portions and pour into the hot pan.

6. Cook the pancake for 5 minutes on one side, flip and cook for an extra 2 minutes.

Nutrition Per Serving

Calories: 309, Fat: 27.1g, Carbohydrates: 2.2g, Protein: 13.4g

LUNCH

Strawberry Spinach Salad
It's flavorful, colorful and yummy.

Servings: 4

Preparation time: 10 minutes

Cooking time: 0 minutes

Ingredients:

<u>For The Salad:</u>

5 ounces of baby spinach

1/4 cup of sliced almonds

1 cup of sliced strawberries

<u>For The Dressing:</u>

1/4 cup of olive or avocado oil

2 tablespoons of red wine vinegar

1/2 teaspoon of vanilla stevia

1/8 teaspoon of garlic powder

1/8 teaspoon of paprika

1/8 teaspoon of salt

Directions:

1. Combine all the salad ingredients in a medium bowl.

2. Whisk the dressing ingredients together and drizzle over the salad.

Nutrition Per Serving

Calories: 75, Fat: 5g, Carbohydrates: 6.3g, Protein: 2.7g

DINNER

Creamy Broccoli &Coconut Soup

Boost your immunity with this nutrient-dense soup.

Servings: 4

Preparation time: 10 minutes

Cooking time: 27 minutes

Ingredients:

4 cups of vegetable broth

3/4 cup of full fat coconut milk

1 head of broccoli, cut into florets

2 shallots, peeled and chopped

2 garlic cloves, peeled and minced

2 tablespoons of virgin coconut oil, divided

2 tablespoons of coconut cream

1/3 teaspoon of salt

1/4 teaspoon of cracked black pepper

A handful of watercress, optional

Directions:

1. In a saucepan, simmer the vegetable broth for 20 minutes over medium heat until half of the broth is absorbed.

2. In another pan, heat a tablespoon of oil over medium heat and sauté the onion for 2 minutes.

3. Add the garlic and sauté for an extra minute. Remove from heat.

4. When the vegetable broth is reduced, add the broccoli florets and bring down from heat. Leave to sit for 10 minutes.

5. Return saucepan to heat; add the sautéed vegetables, milk, salt and pepper. Stir and heat for 1-2 minutes.

6. Transfer the soup to a blender; add the cream, watercress and remaining coconut oil. Blend until smooth.

7. Return soup to saucepan and heat.

Nutrition Per Serving:

Calories: 311, Fat: 29.5g, Carbohydrates: 8g, Protein: 4.8g

DAY 8

BREAKFAST

Vegan Keto-Rich Porridge
Servings: 1

Preparation time: 2minutes

Cooking time: 5minutes

Ingredients

2 tablespoons coconut flour

2 tablespoons vegan vanilla protein powder

3 tbsp of golden flaxseed meal

1½ cups of almond milk, unsweetened

Powdered erythritol, to taste

Directions:

1. Combine the protein powder, golden flaxseed meal as well as coconut flour in a bowl.

2. Transfer to a pan and add the almond milk.

3. Cook over medium heat until it thickens.

4. Add erythritol, to taste and serve with toppings of choice.

Nutrition Per Serving

Calories: 249, Fat: 13.07g, Net Carbohydrates: 5.78g, Protein: 17.82g

LUNCH

Tofu Salad

Servings: 4

Preparation time: 10 minutes

Cooking time:0 minutes

Ingredients

1 block of extra firm tofu, press to remove moisture

1/4 cup celery, finely chopped

1/2 cup vegan maya

1/4 cups of carrots, finely chopped

1/2 teaspoon of kelp powder

1 teaspoon of onion powder

1 teaspoon of lemon juice

Salt &pepper to taste

Celery sticks and for serving

Directions:

1. In a big bowl, combine all ingredients (except seaweed snacks and celery sticks) until well incorporated.

2. Break the seaweed snack over it.

3. Serve salad with celery sticks.

Nutrition Per Serving

Calories: 119, Fat: 5g, Net Carbohydrates: 5g, Protein: 10g.

DINNER

Vegan Carrot Soup
Ingredients

1/ 2 cup carrots, chopped

1/2 cup cauliflower, chopped & peeled

3 cups of vegetable stock

1/4 cup hemp seeds

2tbsp olive oil

2 garlic cloves, minced or 1/2 tsp garlic powder

1/2 tsp onion powder

1 tablespoon of herbs blend such as herbs de provence

Salt and pepper to taste

Directions:

1. Sauté cauliflower, carrots, onions and garlic in heated olive oil for about 5 minutes, stirring often.

2. Pour the vegetable stock over this mixture and keep cooking, until the cauliflower and carrots are soft.

3. Remove from the heat and cool 2-3 minutes and then add the hemp seeds.

4. Blend or puree. *Enjoy!*

Nutrition Per Serving

Calories: 152, Fat: 10.7g, Net Carbohydrates: 5.6g, Protein: 4.1g.

DAY 9

BREAKFAST

Hemp Pumpkin Oatmeal
Start your mornings on the right note with a bowl of oats.

Servings: 1

Preparation time: 2 minutes

Cooking time: 0 minutes

Ingredients:

3 tablespoons of hemp hearts

3 tablespoons of almond milk

1 tablespoon of pumpkin purée

2 drops of liquid stevia

1 teaspoon of chia seeds

1/2 teaspoon of pumpkin pie spice

Directions:

1. Combine all the ingredients thoroughly in a Mason jar or bowl.

2. Cover and refrigerate for at least 4 hours or preferably overnight.

Nutrition Per Serving

Calories: 310, Fat: 27g, Carbohydrates: 3g, Protein: 11g

LUNCH

Cabbage Salad

A healthy Mediterranean inspired dish.

Servings: 6

Preparation time: 10 minutes

Cooking time: 0 minutes

Ingredients:

3 cups of red cabbage, coarsely chopped

3 cups of green cabbage, coarsely chopped

3 tablespoons of lemon juice

1 tablespoon of olive oil

1 teaspoon of cumin

1 teaspoon of black pepper

1 teaspoon of dried mint

1/2 teaspoon of salt

1/2 teaspoon of crushed red pepper flakes

Directions:

1. Combine all the ingredients in a large bowl.

2. Chill for 1 hour at least before serving.

Nutrition Per Serving

Calories: 47, Fat: 2g, Carbohydrates: 6g, Protein: 1g

DINNER

Cream Of Pumpkin Soup

An extremely creamy and velvety soup made with just 4 ingredients.

Servings: 4

Preparation time: 5 minutes

Cooking time: 45 minutes

Ingredients:

2 cups of roasted pumpkin

2 cups of vegetable stock

1/2 cup of cashew cream

1 teaspoon of onion powder

Directions:

1. Add the vegetable stock, onion powder and pumpkin to a large pan. Mix and cook over high heat.

2. Bring to a boil and reduce heat to medium low.

3. Cover the pan and leave to simmer for 30 minutes.

4. Meanwhile, whip the cream until it forms soft peaks, cover and keep in the refrigerator.

5. Blend the soup until smooth after the 30 minutes has elapsed.

6. Pout in the chilled cream and gently whisk to combine.

Nutrition Per Serving

Calories: 209, Fat: 16.7g, Carbohydrates: 7g, Protein: 5.3g

DAY 10

BREAKFAST

Vegan Keto 'Oatmeal'
Servings: 1

Preparation time: 5 minutes

Cooking time: 30minutes

Ingredients:

2 tablespoons flaked coconut

1 tablespoon almond flour

2 tablespoon hemp seeds

1/8 tsp pink Himalayan salt

1 tablespoon chia seeds

1/2 tablespoon whole flax seeds or 1 tbsp ground flax seeds

4 to 6 ounces hot water

1 tablespoon coconut oil

Directions:

1. Add all the ingredients to a pot and bring to a boil. Lower heat and simmer, stirring constantly, until it becomes thick.

2. To thicken more, leave it to rest for 30-60 minutes or eat immediately.

3. To make sweeter, add protein powder of choice to the ingredients.

4. For savory, add desired unsweetened protein powder to the ingredients

5. If meal prepping, add the dry ingredients to a container and cover tightly. When ready to use, add dry content to hot water, stir well, add coconut oil and leave it to thicken for about 5 minutes.

Nutrition Per Serving

Calories: 484, Fat: 36g, Carbohydrates: 4.1g, Protein: 23.3g

LUNCH

Colorful Vegetable Noodles
It is beautiful, fun and perfect for lunch.

Servings: 6

Preparation time: 15 minutes

Cooking time: 20 minutes

Ingredients:

6 ounces of mixed bell peppers, thinly sliced

4 ounces of red onion, thinly sliced

3 large garlic cloves, thinly sliced

4 tablespoons of oil

1 medium summer squash, spiralized

1 medium zucchini, spiralized

1 large carrot, spiralized

Salt

Pepper

Directions:

1. Preheat oven to 400°F.

2. Coat a baking pan with oil.

3. Mix the vegetables together in a bowl and season with a sprinkle of salt and pepper.

4. Transfer the vegetables to the baking pan and spread it out in a thin layer.

5. Bake for 20 minutes. Toss halfway while cooking.

Nutrition Per Serving

Calories: 48, Fat: 0.5g, Carbohydrates: 7g, Protein: 1.5g

DINNER

Eggplant Hash
A North African inspired dish.

Servings: 8

Preparation time: 15 minutes

Cooking time: 15 minutes

Ingredients:

1/2 cup of sun-dried tomatoes in oil, drained and chopped

1/4 cup of toasted slivered almonds

1/4 cup of whole fresh mint leaves

2 tablespoons of light oil

4 garlic cloves, crushed

2 small red bell peppers, seeded and cut into cubes

1 large eggplant globe, peeled, cut into cubes and salted

1 medium red onion, chopped

1/2 teaspoon of ground coriander seed

14 teaspoon of powdered cayenne pepper

Salt

Freshly cracked pepper

Directions:

1. Preheat a large wok or sauté pan over high heat.

2. Add the oil, lift the pan and swirl it to coat with the oil.

3. Sauté the bell peppers and eggplant for about 1 minute. Toss and spread the veggies in the pan for an additional 1 minute so they can sear.

4. Add the garlic and onion; cook for about 2 minutes.

5. Add salt and pepper; toss and spread the vegetables for 1-2 minutes so that they can sear.

6. Add the mint leaves, tomatoes and almonds; toss to combine.

7. Adjust seasoning and add the spices.

8. Give one last stir and serve.

Nutrition Per Serving

Calories: 99.86, Fat: 6.4g, Carbohydrates: 8.9g, Protein: 2.42g

DAY 11

BREAKFAST

Coconut Cocoa Shake

Add some pep to your day with this creamy bomb.

Servings: 1-2

Preparation time: 5 minutes

Cooking time: 0 minute

Ingredients:

6-8 ounces of unsweetened coconut milk

4 ounces of full fat coconut milk or cream

1-2 tablespoons of cocoa powder

1-2 tablespoons of melted coconut oil

1/2 tablespoon of sunflower seeds butter

A dash of sea salt

Directions:

1. Blend all the ingredients together in a blender until smooth.

Nutrition Per Serving

Calories: 220, Fat: 16g, Carbohydrates: 5g, Protein: 3g

LUNCH

Asian Zucchini Salad
A nice, crunchy and filling salad

Servings: 10

Preparation time: 10 minutes

Cooking time: 0 minutes

Ingredients:

1 pound of cabbage, shredded

1 cup of almonds, sliced

1 cup of shelled sunflower seeds

1/3 cup of rice, white or cider vinegar

3/4 cup of avocado oil

1 medium-sized zucchini, spiralized thinly

1 teaspoon of stevia drops

Directions:

1. Use a knife or kitchen shears to chop the zucchini into smaller pieces. Keep aside.

2. Mix the sunflower seeds, cabbage and almonds together in a large bowl.

3. Add the zucchini and stir to combine.

4. Use a fork to whisk the vinegar, stevia and oil in a small bowl.

5. Drizzle the dressing over the salad and toss to coat.

6. Refrigerate for 2 hours before serving.

Nutrition Per Serving

Calories: 120, Fat: 9.3g, Carbohydrates: 7.3g, Protein: 4g

DINNER

Basil Tomato Soup
A spicy soup perfect for winter.

Servings: 6

Preparation time: 10 minutes

Cooking time: 50 minutes

Ingredients:

3 pounds of plum tomatoes, divided

1 quart of vegetable broth

6 garlic cloves, minced

1 sweet onion, chopped

1/2 cup of basil, roughly chopped

3 tablespoons of olive oil, divided

2 tablespoons of tomato paste

2 tablespoons of vegan butter

1 tablespoon of sriracha

1 tablespoon of salt

1 teaspoon of crushed red pepper

1/2 teaspoon of thyme

1/2 teaspoon of pepper

1/2 teaspoon of cayenne

1/2 teaspoon of paprika

Directions:

1. Wash and thoroughly dry 2/3 of the tomatoes, about 8, cut in half lengthwise and place on a greased cookie sheet with the cut side facing up. Chop the remaining tomatoes into small pieces.

2. Sprinkle salt and oil over the tomatoes and roast in the oven for about 40 minutes at 400°F until wrinkly but dark.

3. Meanwhile, heat a tablespoon of oil in a large pot and sauté the garlic and onion until translucent and fragrant.

4. Add the chopped tomatoes and broth, bring to a boil.

5. Add the basil leaves, butter, tomato paste and spices while cooking over medium heat.

6. Add the roasted tomatoes at this point, reduce heat to low and let it simmer for about 40 minutes.

7. Blend the soup in a blender until smooth.

Nutrition Per Serving

Calories: 164, Fat: 12g, Carbohydrates: 9g, Protein: 3g

DAY 12

BREAKFAST

Nut And Seed Granola
Servings: 6- 10 portions

Preparation time: 5 minutes

Cooking time: 10minutes

Ingredients:

1/2 cup pumpkin seeds

1 cup sunflower seeds

1/2 cup dried coconut, shredded

1/4 cup ground flax seed

1/4 cup whole flax seed

Directions:

1. In a pan, toast the sunflower and pumpkin seeds in a preheated skillet on medium high until golden brown, stirring while toasting.

2. Remove pan and add the shredded coconut to it. Add stevia (optional) to sweeten. Stir until sweet to your taste.

3. Add the ground and whole flax, sprinkling in.

4. Set aside to cool and place in an airtight container. Refrigerate or store in the pantry for a month.

LUNCH

Avocado Salsa

Keep hunger at bay with this nourishing recipe.

Servings: 8

Preparation time: 10 minutes

Cooking time: 0 minutes

Ingredients:

4 avocados, peeled and chopped

2 tomatoes, finely chopped

1 fresh chili, finely chopped

1 lemon, juiced

1 red onion, finely chopped

Directions:

Combine all the ingredients in a bowl.

Nutrition Per Serving

Calories: 178, Fat: 14g, Carbohydrates: 5g, Protein: 2g

DINNER

Almond Buttered Shirataki Noodles
A classic dinner dish that's got just the calories you need!

Servings: 1

Preparation time: 8 minutes

Cooking time: 10minutes

Ingredients

1 tbsp coconut oil

2 cloves garlic, minced

3 spring onions, diced

3.5 oz long-stemmed broccoli

1/4 cabbage shredded

1 small carrot, cut into small batons

1 pkg. Shirataki noodles

1 tbsp almond butter

1- 2 tsp sriracha sauce

2 tbsp coconut aminos

Directions:

1. In a large saucepan, heat the olive oil on medium heat and then add the onions and garlic. Cook 2-3 minutes. Once softened, add the remaining vegetables.

2. Remove noodles from packet, rinse with warm water and add to the vegetables on the stove.

3. Once it's almost cooked, stir in the sriracha, almond butter and coconut aminos until warm through.

4. Serve and enjoy!

Nutrition Per Serving

Calories: 190, Fat: 9.9g, Carbohydrates: 12g, Protein: 8.1g

DAY 13

BREAKFAST

Chocolate Chia Smoothie

A super-powerful breakfast recipe that provides you with healthy fats and protein

Servings: 1-2

Preparation time: 5 minutes

Cooking time: minutes

Ingredients:

1-2 cups of organic almond milk

1 tablespoon of raw cacao powder

1 tsp of flax seed

1 tsp of chia seed

1 tablespoon of coconut butter

½ cup of blueberries

1 scoop of high quality protein powder

½ avocado, optional

½ tsp of vanilla, optional

Directions:

1. Add all the ingredients to a blender and blend well.

2. Add liquid and ice to desired thickness.

3. *Enjoy!*

Nutrition Per Serving

Calories: 266, Fat: 15g, Carbohydrates: 8g, Protein: 17g

LUNCH

Nutrient-Dense Avocado Salad

Make this in minutes and get filled up for many hours!

Servings: 2

Preparation time: 5minutes

Cooking time: minutes

Ingredients:

½ small kale bunch

1-2handfuls baby spinach

¼ red onion, diced

2-4 stalks celery, diced

½ red and yellow bell pepper, diced

1 Avocado, cut into chunks

6 oz vegan cheese cut into chunks

For garnish:

½ lemon

2oz of olive oil

Ground or shredded ginger

Oregano, basil & thyme

Directions:

1. Combine all ingredients in a bowl and toss well.

2. Squeeze lemon over it, as well as the herbs and olive oil.

3. Enjoy!

Nutrition Per Serving

Calories: 433, Fat: 39g, Carbohydrates: 12g, Protein: 7g

DINNER

Peanut Sesame Zoodles

Servings: 6

Preparation time: 5minutes

Cooking time: minutes

Ingredients:

For the Sauce:

1/3 cup natural creamy peanut butter

2 tablespoons tamari or soy sauce

1 1/2 tablespoon fresh lime juice (juice of half a lime)

1-inch piece fresh ginger

1 teaspoon toasted sesame oil

1 tsp rice vinegar

1 teaspoon Sriracha or chili sauce of your choice

4-5 Tbsp room temperature water (for adjusting sauce thickness)

For the Zoodle Salad:

3 zucchini, spiralized

2 cups red cabbage, shredded

1/2 large carrot, grated

4 scallions, chopped

¼ cup roasted, unsalted peanuts, chopped

For garnish:

Hemp seeds

Sesame seeds, white or black

Cilantro

Directions:

1. In a blender, add the peanut butter, sesame oil, soy sauce or tamari and chili sauce or Sriracha.

2. Add water to desired consistency (5 tablespoons and above may be too thin).

3. Add the zoodle salad ingredients to a mixing bowl and then add half of the sauce into bowl along with salad components, tossing well.

4. Place the zoodles in bowl. Drizzle the remaining sauce. Garnish bowl with garnish of choice.

Nutrition Per Serving

Calories: 162, Fat: 11g, Carbohydrates: 7.6g, Protein: 6g

DAY 14

BREAKFAST

Peanut Butter Choco Chip Cereal
A satisfying meal that reminds you of old comfort food

Servings: 1/2 cup

Preparation time: 20 minutes

Cooking time: 25minutes

Ingredients

1/2 cup flaxseed meal

1/2 cup almond flour

1/4 cup cacao nibs

2 tbsp peanut butter powder (PB fit)

1/4 cup sugar-free sweetener

1 tbsp coconut oil

1/2 cup water

Directions:

1. Preheat oven to 350°F.

2. In a lined cookie sheet that's been sprayed with cooking spray, combine the flaxmeal, PB fit, almond flour, sweetener and cacao nibs. Add the oil and water, mixing well.

3. Add some oils to your hands and roll into small balls. Place on the lined and sprayed sheet and bake at 350°F for 20 -25 minutes.

4. Turn off oven and let it sit 30 minutes longer. Take out tray and cool.

5. Enjoy plain or with your favorite vegan milk

Nutrition Per Serving

Calories: 212, Fat: 23g, Carbohydrates: 3.2g, Protein: 7g

LUNCH

Crunchy Tofu And Bok Choy Salad

Servings: 3

Preparation time: 20 minutes

Cooking time: 25minutes

Ingredients

For the oven baked tofu:

15 oz extra firm tofu, press dry and chopped into squares

1 tablespoon sesame oil

1 tablespoon soy sauce

2 teaspoons garlic, minced

1 tablespoon water

Juice ½ lemon

1 tablespoon rice wine vinegar

For the Bok Choy Salad:

1 stalk of green onion

9 ounce of bok choy

2 tablespoons cilantro, chopped

1 tablespoon of sambal olek

1 tablespoon of peanut butter

3 tablespoons of coconut oil

Juice ½ lime

2 tablespoons soy sauce

7 drops liquid stevia

Directions:

1. Press the tofu to dry it for 5 to 6 hours.

2. Add the sesame oil, soy sauce, water, vinegar, garlic, and lemon. Place the chopped tofu along with the marinade in a plastic bag. Leave to marinate for overnight, or for at least 30 minutes.

3. Pre-heat oven to 350°F. Place tofu on a lined baking sheet and bake 30 to 35 minutes.

4. In a bowl, combine all the ingredients for salad dressing (except the bok choy). Add the spring onion and cilantro.

5. Make slices of the bok choy by chopping up.

6. Take out the tofu from the oven. Assemble your salad with it, along it with the bok choy, and sauce.

Nutrition Per Serving

Calories: 398.59, Fat: 30.43g, Carbohydrates: 6.68g, Protein: 24.11g

DINNER

Carrot, Cucumber & Radish Slaw
Servings: 2

Preparation time: 15 minutes

Cooking time: 0minutes

Ingredients

8 to10 medium radishes of medium sizes, washed & grated

2 medium carrots, peeled, washed & grated

1/2 cucumber, washed & grated

1 tablespoon of olive oil

½ tbsp Balsamic vinegar

½ tbsp kosher salt

Pepper, to taste

½ teaspoon of low carb sweetener of choice

Directions:

1. Add all grated vegetables to a bowl and then add the rest of the ingredients.

2. Enjoy immediately!

Nutrition Per Serving

Calories: 96, Fat: 6g, Carbohydrates: 6g, Protein: 2g

DAY 15

BREAKFAST

Basic Chia Seed Pudding
It's loaded with fiber, protein and healthy fats, low in sugar and super filling

Servings: 2 cups

Preparation time: 10 minutes

Cooking time: 0 minutes

Ingredients

6 tablespoons chia seeds

2 cups unsweetened coconut or cashew milk

1/2 teaspoon of vanilla extract

Blueberries and strawberries, for topping

Directions:

1. Combine chia seeds, milk and vanilla in a bowl until well mixed.

2. Let it sit 5 minutes, stir once more, cover and refrigerate for 1 to 2 hours.

3 (or prep the night before and let it sit overnight in the refrigerator). To serve, transfer to bowls and top with berries.

Nutrition Per Serving

Calories: 223, Fat: 12g, Carbohydrates: 1g, Protein: 10g

LUNCH

Sesame Tofu & Eggplant
Servings: 4

Preparation time: minutes

Cooking time: minutes

Ingredients

1 pound block firm tofu

1 cup cilantro, chopped

3 tablespoons rice vinegar

4 tablespoons toasted sesame oil

2 cloves garlic, minced finely

1 teaspoon of crushed red pepper flakes

2 teaspoons Swerve sweetener

1 whole (17oz) eggplant, peeled & julienned

1 tablespoon olive oil

Salt and pepper to taste

¼ cup sesame seeds

¼ cup soy sauce

Directions:

1. Preheat oven to 200°F. Dry the tofu by pressing out water from it.

2. In a large bowl, add 3 tablespoons rice vinegar, ¼ cup of cilantro and 2 tablespoons toasted sesame oil. Also add the red pepper flakes, Swerve and minced garlic and whisk together.

3. Add the eggplant to the marinade, mixing well.

4. Now add the olive oil to a skillet and heat on medium-low. Add the eggplant and cook until it becomes soft. Turn the oven off.

5. Next, stir in the cilantro that's left into the eggplant then remove to an oven safe dish. Cover and keep warm in the oven. Wipe out the skillet and place it back to heat up again.

6. Unwrap the tofu, cut it into 8 slices and then spread the sesame seeds on a wide plate. Press the sides of all 8 tofu pieces into the seeds.

7. Next, add 2 tablespoons of the sesame oil to the skillet. Add the tofu and fry 5 minutes per side. Pour in the ¼ cup of soy sauce to and coat tofu pieces. Cook tofu until browned.

8. Remove the eggplant noodles from the oven and put the tofu on top.

Nutrition Per Serving

Calories: 292.75, Fat: 24.45g, Carbohydrates: 6.87g, Protein: 11.21g

DINNER

Vegan Tomato Tart

Servings: 8 slices

Preparation time: 15 minutes

Cooking time: 45 minutes

Ingredients

For The Crust:

3/4 cup of coconut flour

1/2 cup of coconut oil

1/2 tsp salt

1 tbsp ground flax seed + 1/2 cup water

For The Filling:

4 oz of heirloom tomatoes

3 oz vegan cheese substitute

Black pepper, preferred herbs and spices, to taste

Directions:

1. Begin by preheating the oven to 350°F. Combine the crust ingredients and press mixture into pan of about 9 inches. Bake crust until it starts to set, that is for15 to 20 minutes.

2. Remove from the oven and sprinkle the vegan cheese shreds evenly over the crust top.

3. Cut the tomatoes into slices of 1/4 inches and place on top of the cheese. Next, sprinkle the cracked pepper, herbs and spices of choice such as basil and oregano.

4. Cover and bake again for 20 to 25 minutes to melt the cheese and softened the tomatoes.

5. Let it cool for a while, slice and enjoy!

Nutrition Per Serving

Calories: 212.2, Fat: 18g, Carbohydrates: 4.9g, Protein: 2.3g

Day 16

BREAKFAST

Chocolate Avocado Raspberry Smoothie
Gobble your breakfast on the go.

Servings: 2

Preparation time: 3 minutes

Cooking time: 0 minutes

Ingredients:

1 1/4 cup of cashew milk

1/3 cup of frozen raspberries

1/2 avocado

1 tablespoon of powdered sweetener

1 tablespoon of cocoa powder

1/8 teaspoon of raspberry extract

Directions:

Throw all the ingredients into a blender and process until smooth.

Nutrition Per Serving

Calories: 133, Fat: 9.50g, Carbohydrates: 4.84g, Protein: 2.16

LUNCH

Roasted Cauliflower With Cilantro And Lime
The taste is divine!

Servings: 4

Preparation time: 10 minutes

Cooking time: 30 minutes

Ingredients:

1 head of cauliflower, leaves removed and bottom trimmed

2 tablespoons of ground coriander

1/2 lime

1/2 red finger chili, sliced

1 tablespoon of coconut oil, warm

Sprigs of cilantro

Sea salt

Freshly ground black pepper

Directions:

1. Preheat oven to 400°F.

2. Chop the cauliflower into large florets and place on a rimmed baking pan in a single layer.

3. Drizzle the oil over the florets, allow the oil to flow down the sides.

4. Dust the florets with coriander and sprinkle the sea salt over it.

5. Roast in the oven for about 30 minutes until both the top and bottom of the cauliflower is brown.

6. Add the red chilies topping and squeeze the lime juice over it.

7. Add the cilantro on top, season with salt and pepper.

Nutrition Per Serving

Calories: 50, Fat: 6g, Carbohydrates: 2g, Protein: 2g

DINNER

Green Soup With Roasted Toppings
Servings: 2

Preparation time: 10 minutes

Cooking time: 35 minutes

Ingredients:

1 large leek, chopped

4 cups cauliflowers, chopped (blend 3, roast 1 for topping)

4 cups broccolis, chopped (blend 3, roast 1 for topping)

3 ½ cups water

2 cups of kale

1 tablespoon of soy sauce

1 teaspoon of smoked garlic powder

 2 bay leaves

1 teaspoon turmeric

Handful parsley

Sprig of thyme

Directions:

1. Roast the selected vegetables (cauliflower and broccoli) for 15 minutes.

2. While it roasts, steam or boil the chopped broccoli and cauliflower until its tender or for about 10 minutes.

3. Now add the kale, the rest of the ingredients as well as water and let it simmer for another 10 minutes or until the kale is well cooked.

4. Take out the bay leaves and then blend the soup to desired smoothness.

5. Ladle into bowls, top with the roasted vegetable and enjoy.

Nutrition Per Serving

Calories: 189, Fat: 23g, Carbohydrates: 11g, Protein: 14g

Day 17

BREAKFAST

Chai Pumpkin Keto Smoothie

This refreshing breakfast treat contains vanilla bean, pureed pumpkin, chai tea and some good healthy fats.

Servings: 1

Preparation time: 5 minutes

Cooking time: minutes

Ingredients

3 tablespoons pumpkin puree

¾ cup full-fat coconut milk

1 tablespoon MCT oil, optional

1 teaspoon loose chai tea

1 teaspoon of alcohol-free vanilla

½ teaspoon pumpkin pie spice

½ avocado, fresh or frozen

Directions:

1. Add all the ingredients to a blender (except the avocado) and then blend to smoothness.

2. Now add the avocado and blend well.

3. Serve, sprinkled with pumpkin pie spice.

4. (to make your own pumpkin pie spice, combine¼ teaspoon ground cinnamon, 1/8 teaspoon ground nutmeg and1/8 teaspoon ground ginger)

Nutrition Per Serving

Calories: 726, Fat: 69.8 g, Carbohydrates: 11.3g, Protein: 5.5g

LUNCH

Vinaigrette Toasted Green Beans
Simple to prepare.

Servings: 6

Preparation time: 10 minutes

Cooking time: 10 minutes

Ingredients:

1 pound of fresh green beans

1/3 cup of chopped walnuts

1/4 cup of olive oil

2 teaspoons of Dijon mustard

2-3 garlic cloves

Salt

Pepper

Directions:

1. Steam the beans.

2. Meanwhile heat oil in a pan and sauté the garlic for 1 minute.

3. Add the mustard and chopped walnuts to the pan. Cook for an extra 2 minutes until the walnuts are toasted.

4. Drizzle the walnut mixture over the steamed green beans.

5. Season with salt and pepper.

Nutrition Per Serving

Calories: 150.5, Fat: 13.5g, Carbohydrates: 6.7g, Protein: 2.5g

DINNER

Roasted Radishes With Sauce

Servings: 4

Preparation time: minutes

Cooking time: minutes

Ingredients:

20-25 medium radishes

1 1/2 tablespoons of roasted peanut oil

1 1/2 tablespoons of soy sauce

2 green onions, sliced

2-3 tsp. black sesame seeds or white sesame seeds, toasted

Directions:

1. Preheat oven to 425°F. Wash the radishes, trim the ends, and cut into fou pieces or into halves of same sizes.

2. In a sprayed large baking sheet, place the radishes and brush sides with peanut oil, then arrange with the cut side down to brown. Roast the radishes 20-25 minutes, stirring once or twice

3. Once browned, remove the radishes, and brush with the soy sauce and sprinkle with slices of green onions. Return to oven and roast another 5 to 7 minutes.

4. Serve, sprinkled with sesame seeds.

Nutrition Per Serving

Calories: 68, Fat: 6g, Carbohydrates: 1g, Protein: 1g

Day 18

BREAKFAST

Carrot Cake Chia Pudding

This super easy, protein-packed recipe is so filling and nutritious, and a fun way to start the day!

Servings: 2-4

Preparation time: 10 minutes

Cooking time: 0 minutes

Ingredients

2 cups of almond milk

2-3 tablespoons sweetener

2 teaspoons of pure vanilla extract

1 large carrot (1 cup), peeled & roughly chopped

¼ to ½ teaspoon of cinnamon

2 large pinches sea salt

½ cup of chia seeds

Directions:

1. Add the milk, vanilla extract, sweetener, carrot, cinnamon and salt to a blender. Blend until smooth.

2. Combine the chia seeds and almond milk in a bowl, stir and let it sit 3 minutes.

3. Now stir mixture with a fork to combine everything well and then refrigerate for an hour.

4. Serve with toppings of choice. This could be raisins, walnuts, shredded coconut or carrot strips.

Nutrition Per Serving

Calories: 156, Fat: 7g, Carbohydrates: 5g, Protein: 7g

LUNCH

Spicy Spaghetti Squash
Servings: 3

Preparation time: 15 minutes

Cooking time: 65minutes

Ingredients

1 medium spaghetti squash, cut in half, lengthwise and seeded

2 garlic cloves, minced

1 small tomato, sliced

1 handful basil, finely chopped

3 tbsp extra virgin olive oil

Pink salt and black pepper

Directions:

1. Preheat oven to 375°F. Add the spaghetti squash and bake for 60 minutes. Remove once it can be pierced easily through with a paring knife. Side aside for10 minutes to cool.

2. Scrape the squash with a fork so it can bring out long, spaghetti-like strands.

3. Heat up pan with oil, add the garlic and tomato and sauté over medium-low heat for 2-3 minutes.

4. Add the basil, salt, pepper, as well as the spaghetti squash, into tomato-garlic mix.

5. Add vegan butter to taste, if using

Nutrition Per Serving

Calories: 158, Fat: 17g, Carbohydrates: 1g, Protein: 1g

DINNER

Mediterranean Zoodles Pasta
It's fast and easy to prepare.

Servings: 4

Preparation time: 10 minutes

Cooking time: 13 minutes

Ingredients:

1 cup of packed spinach

1/4 cup of sun-dried tomatoes

2 tablespoons of Italian flat leaf parsley, chopped

2 tablespoons of vegan butter

2 tablespoons of capers

2 tablespoons of olive oil

10 kalamata olives, halved

5 garlic cloves, minced

2 large zucchinis, spiralized

Sea salt

Black pepper

Directions:

1. Cook the spinach, zucchini, salt, oil, pepper, garlic and butter in a large pot over medium heat until the spinach wilts and the zucchini softens. Drain the excess liquid.

2. Add the capers, tomatoes, olives and parsley. Stir and cook for 2-3 minutes.

Nutrition Per Serving

Calories: 231, Fat: 20g, Carbohydrates: 6.5g, Protein: 6.5g

DAY 19

BREAKFAST

Vanilla Chia pudding
Servings: 2

Preparation time: 10 minutes

Cooking time: 0 minutes

Ingredients:

6 tbsp chia seeds

2 cups fresh almond milk

3 tablespoons of date paste or liquid sweetener of choice

2 tsp pure vanilla extract

2 large pinches cinnamon (optional)

1 large pinch of Himalayan crystal salt or sea salt

Directions:

1. Combine all the ingredients in a bowl, stirring well. Let it sit 4 minutes.

2. Stir until mixed and refrigerate for an hour.

3. Serve with chopped nuts

Nutrition Per Serving

Calories: 434, Fat: 11g, Carbohydrates: 5g, Protein: 11 g

LUNCH

Thai Coconut Curry Soup
A delicious vegetable-dense Thai coconut curry soup spooned over zucchini noodles.

Servings: 8

Preparation time: 15 minutes

Cooking time: 40 minutes

Ingredients:

4 tablespoons of coconut oil

4 cloves garlic

1 medium onion

10 slices (¼" thick) fresh ginger

4 tablespoons of red Thai curry paste

6 cups of veggie broth

1-13.5 oz. can coconut milk

1 red bell pepper, halved, seeded & sliced

8 oz. white mushrooms

3-4 tbsp. fresh lime juice

2 cups of cauliflower florets

1 tablespoon of Vegan Fysh Sauce

3 green onions, sliced

¼ cup of cilantro, chopped

2 large zucchinis, spiralized

Directions:

1. Add coconut oil to pan and melt. Add onion, ginger, garlic, and Thai curry paste. Stir and cook for 5 to 7 minutes.

2. Once the onions start softening, add the veggie broth and bring to a boil. Set heat to low and simmer for 20 minutes.

3. Remove and pass mixture through a strainer into a bowl. Return only the broth to the pan, while discarding the aromatics.

4. Whisk in the coconut milk and then add bell pepper and mushrooms. Let it simmer about 15 minutes over medium heat until red pepper is softened.

5. Now add the Vegan Fysh Sauce and lime juice, stirring well to combine.

6. Add the spiralized zucchini (zoodles) and place in bowl. Spoon soup over it.

7. Serve, garnished with cilantro and green onions.

Nutrition Per Serving

Calories: 234, Fat: 20.4g, Carbohydrates: 10, Protein: 2g

DINNER

Egg Roll In A Bowl
Besides being keto and vegan, this healthy recipe is nut-free, paleo and full of flavor.

Servings: 2

Preparation time: 5minutes

Cooking time: 15 minutes

Ingredients:

1 tablespoon of olive oil

1/2 red onion, sliced thinly

2 carrots (about 1 cup), shredded

2 celery stalks, chopped

4 cups cabbage, shredded

1 cup mushrooms, sliced

2 tablespoons tamari

1/4 teaspoon fine sea salt

Freshly ground black pepper, to taste

1 teaspoon toasted sesame oil

For garnish: Chopped green onions and sesame seeds,

Directions:

1. In a deep skillet, heat the olive oil over medium-high heat. Add the onion, celery and carrot and sauté about 5 minutes until soft.

2. Add the shredded cabbage, sliced mushrooms, tamari, salt and pepper as well as a little water to prevent sticking.

3. Cover the pan, lower heat and cook10 to 15 minutes until the veggies are tender or to desired consistency.

4. Add the sesame oil and stir. Season with salt and pepper, top with green onions and enjoy!

Nutrition Per Serving

Calories: 231, Fat: 13g, Carbohydrates: 13g, Protein: 8g

DAY 20

BREAKFAST

Chocolate Pumpkin Cookies
Enjoy with a warm glass of milk.

Servings: 20

Preparation time: 10 minutes

Cooking time: 15 minutes

Ingredients:

1 cup of almond butter

1/2 cup of dark chocolate chips, optional

1/2 cup of pumpkin purée

2 teaspoons of pumpkin pie spice

1/4 teaspoon of sea salt

1/4 cup of maple syrup

1 teaspoon of vanilla extract

Directions:

1. Preheat oven to 350°F.

2. Line two baking pans with silpat or parchment paper.

3. In a medium bowl, mix all the ingredients together to form a smooth batter.

4. Fold in the chocolate chips, if using.

5. Drop the batter on the prepared baking pan with a spoon and spread out in circles with the back of the spoon.

6. Bake for 12-15 minutes until the cookies' edges are a bit golden.

Nutrition Per Serving

Calories: 95, Fat: 7g, Carbohydrates: 7g, Protein: 3g

LUNCH

Roasted Cauliflower Vegan Salad
Easy and delicious recipe to try

Servings: 2

Preparation time: 10 minutes

Cooking time: 35minutes

Ingredients:

1 head cauliflower, cut into florets

3 cloves garlic

5 tbsp olive oil

1 lemon

Himalayan salt

2 tbsp walnuts

Half avocado, sliced

1 tbsp Green onion

Black pepper, to garnish

Directions:

1. Preheat oven to 425°F.

2. Add florets to baking sheet and also add 2 chopped garlic cloves, 3 tablespoons of olive oil salt, and drizzle lemon over.

3. Roast 35-40 minutes, tossing infrequently.

4. Meanwhile, prepare your dressing with 2 tbsp of olive oil, 1 tbsp of lemon juice, salt/pepper as well as 1 garlic clove.

5. Once cauliflower is cooked, place on a plate adding nuts of choice, dressing, sliced avocado and green onion.

Nutrition Per Serving

Calories: 564, Fat: 52g, Carbohydrates: 14g, Protein: 8g

DINNER

One-Pot Vegan Mac And Cheese

Servings: 4

Preparation time: 5 minutes

Cooking time: 20minutes

Ingredients:

1 tbsp coconut oil

1/4 tsp garlic salt

1/4 cup almond meal

1/4 tsp fresh-ground pepper

1 head cauliflower

1 (4 oz) jar baby food carrots

1 (15 oz) can coconut milk

2 tbsp cashew butter or 1 tbsp tahini

1 tbsp olive oil

1 1/2 tsp onion powder

3/4 tsp ground mustard

1/2 tsp sea salt

1/2 tsp pepper

1 tbsp fresh parsley, chopped (optional)

Directions:

1. Add coconut to a large pan and melt over medium-high heat. Add the almond meal along with the garlic salt, and pepper. Cook the almond meal to show some taste and then remove to a bowl; setting aside.

2. Now create rectangle pieces that are shaped like macaroni by cutting the cauliflower into pieces of 1/2-inch then into strips of 1/2-inch strips. (Do not bother if the florets crumble).

3. Place the cauliflower in a pan and then carrots, tahini or cashew butter, coconut milk, olive oil, ground mustard, onion powder salt and pepper. Closed lid and cook for 10 minutes or until boiling.

4. Uncover, and keep cooking until cauliflower is tender and sauce begins to thicken. Sprinkle with parsley and some almond meal "breadcrumbs".

Nutrition Per Serving

Calories: 229, Fat: 18g, Carbohydrates: 10g, Protein: 6g

DAY 21

BREAKFAST

Cucumber Vegan Smoothies
A super filling breakfast meal

Servings: 1

Preparation time: 5minutes

Cooking time: 0minutes

Ingredients:

1 cup unsweetened plant milk

1/2 avocado

3 inch piece of cucumber

Small handful berries (optional)

1 teaspoon to 1 tablespoon oil (optional)

1-2 tablespoons protein powder (optional)

Berry flavored syrup, to taste

Directions:

1. Add all the ingredients to a blender and blend to smoothness.

2. Taste and add more berry syrup, if desired.

3. With the berries, it's has 10 gram net carbs, but without them it's about 4 to 5 gram.

Nutrition Per Serving

Calories: 231, Fat: 20g, Carbohydrates: 10g, Protein: 9g

LUNCH

Broccoli Soup

Servings: 4

Preparation time: 10 minutes

Cooking time: 30 minutes

Ingredients:

1 can of full fat coconut milk

3 cups of chopped broccoli florets

3 cups of chopped celery

2 cups of vegetable broth

1/2 teaspoon of garlic pepper

1/2 teaspoon of onion powder

Red pepper flakes

Salt

Pepper

Directions:

1. Add the milk, broccoli, celery, broth, garlic pepper, onion powder and red pepper flakes to a pot. Cook for about 30 minutes over medium heat until the broccoli and celery softens.

2. Pour the soup into a blender and process until smooth.

Nutrition Per Serving

Calories: 200, Fat: 17g, Carbohydrates: 5g, Protein: 4g

7|8|18 ✓ good

DINNER

Vegan Keto Lo Mein

The delicious vegan keto version of your classic Lo Mein.

Servings: 1 large bowl

Preparation time: 10minutes

Cooking time: 5minutes

Ingredients:

1 pkg. kelp noodles or shitraki noodles

1/4 cup of carrots, julienned

1/2 cup edamame, shelled

1/4 cup mushrooms, sliced

1 cup of frozen spinach

Directions:

For the sauce:

2 tablespoons of tamari (or regular soy sauce or coconut aminos)

1 tablespoon of sesame oil

1/2 teaspoon ginger, ground

1/2 teaspoon garlic powder

1/4 teaspoon sriracha or chili of choice

Directions:

1. Open and soak your preferred noodles in water.

2. Add sauce ingredients, vegetables and edamame to pan and toss on medium heat.

3. Drain the noodles of water and add to pan, simmer 2-3 minutes with occasional stir to enable the noodles soften and take in the sauce. Add some water to pan, if necessary, so keep the contents from burning.

4. Once noodles is soft, stir together to mix in all the ingredients. Turn heat off but keep the noodles in the pan to absorb the liquid that is in the bottom.

5. Serve noodles and enjoy!

Nutrition Per Serving

Calories: 139, Fat: 6g, Carbohydrates: 4.9g, Protein: 7.8g

DAY 22

BREAKFAST

Breakfast Chia Strawberry Jars
Begin your day with a dose of energy.

Servings: 4

Preparation time: 15 minutes

Cooking time: 5 minutes

Ingredients:

1 cup of coconut milk

1 cup of strawberries, sliced

1 cup of coconut milk yogurt

4 tablespoons of whole chia seeds

2 tablespoons of water

1/4 teaspoon of ground ginger

1/4 teaspoon of cinnamon

4 large strawberries, sliced

Liquid stevia, optional

Directions:

1. Cook the 1 cup of strawberry slices with 2 tablespoons of water in a small pan. Simmer and cook for some minutes until it softens. Use either a

spatula or fork to break the strawberries, add a few drops of stevia if using and set aside.

2. Combine the ginger, chia seeds, milk, some drops of stevia and cinnamon in a small bowl. Keep aside for 20-30 minutes to soak. Then evenly divide the mixture between 4 jars.

3. Add the cooked strawberries, followed by the sliced strawberries. Ensure that you press it down firmly to the jar sides.

4. Add the coconut milk yogurt as topping.

Nutrition Per Serving

Calories: 230, Fat: 17.9g, Carbohydrates: 7.5g, Protein: 8.7g

LUNCH

Dill Cucumber Salad
The combination of flavors in this salad gives it a distinct taste.

Servings: 4

Preparation time: 10 minutes

Cooking time: 0 minutes

Ingredients:

1/4 cup of sprig dill

2 cucumbers, cut into 1/4-inch slices

8 tablespoons of white wine vinegar

2 teaspoons of sweetener

1 teaspoon of salt

Directions:

1. In a medium-sized bowl, mix the dill, vinegar, sweetener and salt together.

2. Add the cucumber and toss gently.

3. Keep in the refrigerator for 30 minutes so that the flavors can come together.

4. Drain any extra liquid and serve.

Nutrition Per Serving

Calories: 24, Fat: 0.2g, Carbohydrates: 5g, Protein: 1g

DINNER

Sumac Tempeh With Braised Cauliflower
A warm bowl of Middle Eastern flavors

Servings: 8

Preparation time: 7 minutes

Cooking time: 35 minutes

Ingredients:

For the Sumac Tempeh:

16 oz tempeh (2 pkg.), cut in strips

1 tablespoon of sumac

1/4 cup Lime juice

2 teaspoon of cumin

Pinch Salt and pepper

1 teaspoon of turmeric

4 garlic cloves, minced

1 tbsp olive oil

For the Braised Cauliflower:

1/2 cup (1/2 small onion) yellow onion, diced

1 tablespoon of olive oil

3 garlic cloves, minced

4 cups diced tomatoes (2 large cans)

6 cups cauliflower, cut into 2 inch pieces

2 tbsp fresh thyme, chopped

1/2 teaspoon of coriander

1 teaspoon of cumin

1/2 teaspoon of allspice

Pinch of salt

Directions:

1. In a dish, place in the tempeh strips and cover with lime juice and all the spices including the salt and pepper. Coat the tempeh with the marinade and chill for 20-35 minutes for maximum infusion.

2. Sauté garlic in heated olive oil until golden and set to one side. Transfer the tempeh to the pan and brown per side for 5-6 minutes. Cover pan, lower heat and cook 30 minutes.

3. For the braised cauliflower, sauté onion and garlic in heated olive oil until caramelized.

4. Add in the tomatoes, cauliflower, herbs and spices and stir to combine well.. Cover pot and cook 10 minutes or thereabouts.

5. Top the cooked cauliflower with the pieces of tempeh and drizzle with tahini sprinkle also with sautéed garlic and herbs.

Nutrition Per Serving

Calories: 198, Fat: 11g, Carbohydrates: 12g, Protein: 13g

DAY 23

BREAKFAST

Coconut Macadamia Cocoa Smoothie
It can also serve as a dessert.

Servings: 1

Preparation time: 5 minutes

Cooking time: 0 minutes

Ingredients:

1 cup of ice cubes

3/4 cup of unsweetened coconut milk

2 tablespoons of sweetener

2 tablespoons of salted macadamia nuts, minced

1 tablespoon of unsweetened cocoa powder

1/2 teaspoon of vanilla extract

A dash of salt

Optional toppings:

Toasted coconut

Macadamia nuts

Directions:

1. Blend all the ingredients in a blender until smooth.

2. Add the toppings if desired and serve.

Nutrition Per Serving

Calories: 412.46, Fat: 44.76g, Carbohydrates: 8.04g, Protein: 5.22g

LUNCH

Jackfruit Blend
Servings: 3

Preparation time: minutes

Cooking time: 0 minutes

Ingredients:

1 can of young jackfruit in water

1 tablespoon of chili powder

1 cup of kale

1 package cauliflower rice

1 tablespoon of olive oil

Garlic & onion powder to taste

Vegan cheese for serving

Directions:

1. Drain jackfruit can and chop into pieces.

2. In a pot, add all ingredients except the vegan cheese, stir continuously to incorporate well and sauté until the cauliflower is tender.

3. Enjoy with plain avocado and vegan cheese.

Nutrition Per Serving

Calories: 228, Fat: 8g, Carbohydrates: 6g, Protein: 13g

DINNER

Spicy Puerto Rican Cabbage Salad

Servings: 6

Preparation time: 15minutes

Cooking time: 0 minutes

Ingredients:

5-6 cups green cabbage, finely chopped

1 cup tomatoes, diced

1/2 cup celery, sliced

1/2 cup chopped celery leaves, optional

6 radishes, stem & root cut & cut into crescent slices

1/4 cup of sliced green onions, dark green part

Dressing Ingredients:

2 tablespoons of apple cider vinegar

1teaspoon fresh lime juice

1/2 teaspoon salt

1/4-1/2 teaspoon hot sauce

3 tablespoons of grapeseed oil

Directions:

1. Place all the salad ingredients in a large bowl and toss well.

2. In another bowl, combine the fresh lime juice, apple cider vinegar, hot sauce and salt. Add the oil, whisking in the oil, one tablespoon at a time. Taste it and add more hot sauce, if necessary.

3. Toss salad with dressing. Enjoy immediately or even better, after refrigerating for a few hours.

Nutrition Per Serving

Calories: 120, Fat: 8g, Carbohydrates: 9g, Protein: 3g

DAY 24

BREAKFAST

Peanut Butter Pancakes
Servings: 2

Preparation time: 3minutes

Cooking time: 10 minutes

Ingredients:

4 tablespoons coconut cream

4 tablespoons golden flaxseed

2 tablespoons ground flaxseed

2 tablespoons peanut butter

2 tablespoons sweetener

½ teaspoon baking powder

1 tablespoon coconut oil

Directions:

1. In a bowl, combine all ingredients. Grease pan lightly with oil and heat on medium low.

2. Once hot, add batter and cook until the sides are hard and the tops begin to bubble.

3. Flip and cook 1 to 2 minutes longer.

4. Serve, topped with vegan butter, if desired.

Nutrition Per Serving

Calories: 394.5, Fat: 34.41g, Carbohydrates: 5.39g, Protein: 13.76g

LUNCH

Marinated Mushrooms
Pleases the palate quite well.

Servings: 4

Preparation time: 15 minutes

Cooking time: 5 minutes

Ingredients:

1 pound of cremini mushrooms

2 garlic cloves, crushed

1/4 cup of red onion, chopped

1/4 cup of white wine vinegar

1/4 cup of olive oil

2 tablespoons of fresh parsley leaves, chopped

2 teaspoons of packed brown sugar

1 bay leaf

1/2 teaspoon of whole black peppercorns

1/2 teaspoon of dried oregano

1/4 teaspoon of crushed red pepper flakes

Freshly ground black pepper

Kosher salt

Directions:

1. Bring a large pot of salted water to boil and add the mushrooms. Cook for about 3-4 minutes until it is just soft. Drain.

2. Mix the mushrooms with the peppercorns, garlic, olive oil, onion, pepper flakes, sugar, bay leaf, vinegar and oregano in a bowl. Add salt and pepper to season.

3. Put in an airtight container and refrigerate for 8 hours at least, or up to 5 days.

4. Garnish with parsley and serve at room temperature.

Nutrition Per Serving

Calories: 164.6, Fat: 13.8g, Carbohydrates: 8.9g, Protein: 3.1g

DINNER

Almond Vegetable Mix
Made for busy weeknights.

Servings: 2

Preparation time: 10 minutes

Cooking time: 2 minutes

Ingredients:

For the dressing:

2 tablespoons of extra virgin olive oil

1 tablespoon of organic lemon juice

6 basil leaves, minced

1 garlic clove, minced

1 teaspoon of white vinegar

1/2 teaspoon of black pepper

1/2 teaspoon of Himalayan salt

For the salad:

1 cup of baby spinach

1 cup of spring mix leaves

5 cherry tomatoes

4 asparagus, stem discarded, cut in half

2 radish leaves, sliced

1/4 yellow bell pepper, sliced

1/4 cucumber, sliced

2 tablespoons of almond ricotta cheese

Directions:

1. Combine all the dressing ingredients in a small bowl. Set aside.

2. Boil water in a small pot and cook the asparagus for 4 minutes. Drain.

3. Combine the spring mix and spinach in a large bowl, add the radish, cucumber, bell pepper, asparagus sticks, and cherry tomatoes. Top with the almond cheese.

4. Drizzle the dressing over the salad.

Nutrition Per Serving

Calories: 208, Fat: 18.38g, Carbohydrates: 9.26g, Protein: 4.4g

DAY 25

BREAKFAST

Blueberry Banana-Flavored Bread Smoothie

This banana flavored smoothie gives a good hearty satisfying feeling that is just perfect for breakfast.

Servings: 2

Preparation time: 10minutes

Cooking time: 0minutes

Ingredients:

1 tbsp of chia seeds

3 tablespoons of golden flaxseed meal

10 drops of liquid Stevia

2 cups vanilla coconut milk, unsweetened

2 tablespoons MCT oil

¼ cup blueberries

¼ teaspoon xanthan gum

1 ½ teaspoons of banana extract

Directions:

1. In a blend, add all ingredients.

2. Give it a few minutes to soak and then blend well to incorporate everything.

3. Serve and enjoy!

Nutrition Per Serving

Calories: 270, Fat: 23.31g, Carbohydrates: 4.66g, Protein: 3.13g

LUNCH

Cauliflower Fried Rice With 'Eggs'
Use your cauliflower to make this quick and enjoyable lunch dish

Servings: 2

Preparation time: 15minutes

Cooking time: 15minutes

Ingredients:

1 medium head of cauliflower, cut into florets

1 tablespoon of olive oil

100g Vegan Egg (Follow Your Heart)

Salt, pepper, paprika powder to taste

1 pinch of garlic powder

Directions:

1. Steam the florets 10-15 minutes over boiling water.

2. Once softened, add one at a time, to a food processor and pulse until it looks like flaky rice.

3. Add olive oil to pan; heat on medium and add the garlic powder.

4. Prepare the vegan egg as directed on the package and then add it to the hot pan.

5. Scramble and cook and then add the cauliflower rice, while keep scrambling until the vegan egg is firmed.

6. Season with the paprika powder, salt and pepper. Serve and Enjoy!

Nutrition Per Serving

Calories: 226, Fat: 43g, Carbohydrates: 12.6g, Protein: 11g

DINNER

Roasted Garlic Cauliflower Soup
This has just the right amount of aromatic flavors.

Servings: 6

Preparation time: 10 minutes

Cooking time: 1 hour

Ingredients:

6 cups of vegetable stock

1 large head of cauliflower, chopped

3 shallots, chopped

2 garlic bulbs, peeled

1 tablespoon of extra virgin olive oil

3/4 teaspoon of sea salt

Freshly ground pepper

Directions:

1. Preheat oven to 400°F.

2. Chop off about 1/4-in from the top of the peeled garlic, set it on a piece of aluminum foil and coat each of the garlic with 1/ teaspoon of oil.

3. Roast for 35 minutes. Leave to cool a bit, remove the foil and squeeze out the garlic from its cloves.

4. In the meantime, heat the remaining oil in a medium pan and sauté the shallots for about 6 minutes until it is soft and starts to brown.

5. Add the garlic and the rest of the ingredients, cover and give it time to boil.

6. Lower heat to low and simmer the soup until the cauliflower is soft, for 15-20 minutes.

7. Transfer soup to blender or food processor and process for about 30 seconds until smooth.

8. Adjust seasoning if desired.

Nutrition Per Serving

Calories: 73, Fat: 2.4g, Carbohydrates: 9.2g, Protein: 2.1g

DAY 26

BREAKFAST

Blackberry Chocolate Shake

Servings: 1

Preparation time: 10minutes

Cooking time: 0minutes

Ingredients:

7 ice cubes

1 cup unsweetened coconut milk

2 tablespoons cocoa powder

¼ cup blackberries

12 drops liquid Stevia

2 tablespoons MCT oil

¼ teaspoon xanthan gum

Directions:

1. In a blender, add all ingredients.

2. Give it a few minutes to soak and then blend well to incorporate everything.

3. Serve and enjoy!

Nutrition Per Serving

Calories: 346, Fat: 34.17g, Carbohydrates: 4.8g, Protein: 2.62g

LUNCH

Buffalo Cauliflower Wings
A much healthier version of the classic American recipe.

Servings: 8

Preparation time: 10 minutes

Cooking time: 30 minutes

Ingredients:

For the sauce:

4 tablespoons of hot sauce

2 garlic cloves, minced

2 tablespoons of coconut oil

A pinch of sea salt

For the wings:

4 cups of cauliflower florets, cut into bite-sized pieces

1/2 cup of filtered water

1/2 cup of almond flour

1 tablespoon of hot sauce

2 teaspoons of seasoned salt

Directions:

1. Heat all the sauce ingredients in a small pot.

2. Preheat oven to 450°F.

3. Use parchment paper to line a baking pan.

4. In a bowl, mix the flour and salt thoroughly. Keep aside.

5. In another bowl, mix the hot sauce and water. Combine this mixture with the flour mixture.

6. Coat the florets in the batter mixture and place on the baking pan.

7. Put pan in the middle rack and bake for 25-30 minutes until crisp.

8. Drizzle baked florets with the sauce and serve.

Nutrition Per Serving

Calories: 65, Fat: 3g, Carbohydrates: 8g, Protein: 1g

DINNER

Creamy Coconut Noodles With Spicy Tofu
Servings: 4

Preparation time: 20minutes

Cooking time: 50minutes

Ingredients:

For The Noodles:

2 pkg. shirataki noodles

1 can full fat coconut milk

4 tablespoons of sesame seeds

Juice and zest of 1 lime

1/2 tsp ginger, ground or fresh

1/4 tsp red pepper flakes

Pinch of salt

 For The Tofu:

4 tablespoons low sodium tamari

1 block extra firm tofu, drained with excess moisture pressed out

1 tablespoon olive oil

1/4 tsp of any ground chili pepper

Directions:

1. Preheat your oven to 350°F

2. Cube the drained and dry tofu into blocks of about 1 by 1inches.

3. Combine the chili pepper, tamari and olive oil in a bowl and in another dish, place the tofu cubes in one layer and pour over the tamari mixture. Ensure that are evenly coated by flipping the pieces a couple of times.

4. On a baking sheet, place the tofu pieces and bake 20 to 25 minutes.

5. Next, drain the noodles and rinse and then add to a pan. Add the remaining noodle ingredients as well and mix to combine well.

6. Cover partially and cook 10 minutes; lower the heat and keep cooking another 10 minutes.

7. Once the tofu is done, turn heat off. Set everything (tofu and noodles) aside to cool for some time.

8. Serve, garnished with choice garnishing such as sesame seeds, lime zest and red pepper flakes,

Nutrition Per Serving

Calories: 374.3, Fat: 1.13g, Carbohydrates: 7g, Protein: 15.7g

DAY 27

BREAKFAST

Cashew Yogurt "Sundae"
The quickest and healthiest breakfast ever!

Servings: 1

Preparation time: 3minutes

Cooking time: 0minutes

Ingredients:

2/3 cup of low carb vegan cashew yogurt

1 tbsp of hemp seeds

1/4 cup sliced strawberries

1 tbsp chia

Directions:

1. Pour your vegan cashew yoghurt into a bowl.

2. Add the rest of the ingredients to top.

3. Enjoy your breakfast!

Nutrition Per Serving

Calories: 165, Fat: 9g, Carbohydrates:4g, Protein:12g

LUNCH

Kelp Noodle Pad Thai

Servings: 4

Preparation time: 5minutes

Cooking time: 10minutes

Ingredients

2 bags of kelp noodles

<u>For The Sauce:</u>

1/2 cup extra virgin oil

1tablespoon of poppy seeds

1/4 cup lemon juice

1 teaspoon grated or powdered ginger

1/4 teaspoon salt

Directions:

1. In a jar, add the sauce ingredients together, seal and shake well.

2. Prepare kelp noodles according to instructions.

3. Pour prepared sauce over and enjoy!

Nutrition Per Serving

Calories: 255, Fat: 29g, Carbohydrates: 2g, Protein: 0g

DINNER

One Pot Zucchini Pasta

Servings: 4

Preparation time: 10 minutes

Cooking time: 10 minutes

Ingredients

2 lb zucchini, spiralized

1 pint cherry tomatoes, halved

1 large red onion, sliced thinly

4 cloves of garlic, minced

1/2 cup fresh basil

1/4 cup extra virgin olive oil

1/2 teaspoon crushed red pepper (optional)

Salt & pepper, to taste

Directions:

1. In a large pot, add the olive oil and warm over low to medium heat. Add the onion and garlic, cook until fragrant (3 minutes).

2. To the pot, add the zucchini noodles, add salt and pepper and then cover and let it cook for 2 minutes, while stirring half way through the cooking.

4. Now add the tomatoes and cook 3-4 more minutes, stirring every 30 seconds or so.

5. Once cooked to desired consistency, add the fresh basil and crushed red pepper (if using), then stir to mix well. Serve, garnished with fresh basil.

Nutrition Per Serving

Calories: 181, Fat: 13.3g, Carbohydrates: 11g, Protein: 4.3g

DAY 28

BREAKFAST

Vegan Breakfast Porridge
Meal- prep a batch if this and enjoy stress-free breakfast for a week

Servings: 1

Preparation time: 3 minutes

Cooking time: 5 minutes

Ingredients:

1/2 cup of water

2 tablespoons of almond flour

2 tablespoons of hemp hearts

2 tablespoons of unsweetened coconut, shredded

1 tablespoon of chia seeds

1 tablespoon of flaxseed meal

1/2 teaspoon of pure vanilla extract

1/4 teaspoon of granulated stevia

A pinch of sea salt

Directions:

1. In a small pan, add all the ingredients except the vanilla and stir over low heat.

2. Cook and stir for about 3-5 minutes until it becomes thick.

3. Add the vanilla, stir and serve warm.

Nutrition Per Serving

Calories: 334, Fat: 29g, Carbohydrates: 2g, Protein: 15g

LUNCH

Cauliflower Steak
Super-tasty and delicious!

Servings: 4

Preparation time: 35minutes

Cooking time: 15minutes

Ingredients:

1 medium sized cauliflower, sliced

2 tablespoons of soy sauce

1 teaspoon liquid smoke

1/4 tsp pepper

2 tablespoons of peanut flour

1 1/2 tablespoons of peanut butter

1 tsp soy sauce (for the sauce)

Salt & pepper to taste

1/4 tsp ginger powder

1 tsp lemon juice

Cold water

Hot Sauce, optional

Sesame seeds, for topping

Directions:

1. Wash and slice the cauliflower from the middle.

2. In a bowl, add the soy sauce, pepper and liquid smoke, mix well and then add the sliced cauliflower to the marinade for 30-50 minutes.

3. Roll the steak in the peanut flour, and then fry on both sides in olive oil until browned.

4. To make the peanut sauce, combine peanut butter, hot sauce, ginger powder, pepper, salt, lemon juice in a bowl and whisk well. Add some water slowly and keep whisking until sauce is thickened.

5. Drizzle the peanut sauce over the steak and top with sesame seeds. Enjoy!

Nutrition Per Serving

Calories: 104, Fat: 3g, Carbohydrates: 11g, Protein: 7g

DINNER

Vegan Ramen

Servings: 1

Preparation time: 15minutes

Cooking time: 15minutes

Ingredients:

<u>For the noodles and broth:</u>

1 tbsp sesame oil

2 tbsp coconut aminos or tamari

2 cups vegetable stock

1 garlic clove, minced

I pkg. Shiratki noodles

<u>For the toppings:</u>

1/4 blocked baked tofu (cubed, marinated in tamari and baked 30 min.)

Handful baby spinach

Handful sprouts

1/4 cup mixed mushrooms, sautéed

<u>Garnish:</u>

Chopped scallion

Chili flakes

Seaweed flakes

Sesame seeds

Directions:

1. Sauté garlic and ginger in hot oil until fragrant. Add in the broth and tamari or aminos coconut and let it simmer.

2. Drain noodles, rinse and add to the broth. Simmer for 5-10 minutes.

3. With spoon or fork, carefully take out the noodles from the broth and place in bowl and then place desired toppings over it.

4. Pour broth carefully over the toppings and garnish as desired.

Nutrition Per Serving

Calories: 283, Fat: 18.9g, Carbohydrates: 7g, Protein: 16.5g

DAY 29

BREAKFAST

Keto Vegan Quiche

Enjoy the vegan variation of this French recipe. It tastes divine!

Servings: 5

Preparation time: 10minutes

Cooking time: 35minutes

Ingredients:

1 low carb crust

11/2 cups zucchini, chopped

1 leek (about 3 oz)

2 tablespoons of olive oil

½ teaspoon of salt

14 ounce firm tofu

3-4 tbsp water

1/ tsp turmeric black pepper to taste

Directions:

1. Preheat oven to 356°F, add the oil and fry the veggies

2. In a bowl, add the tofu, water, turmeric, pepper and salt and bend well with a batter.

3. Add the fried vegetables to the tofu mixture and spoon over the crust

4. Bake for 30 minutes and remove once centre is set. Cool 5 minutes then slice and enjoy

Nutrition Per Serving (per slice)

Calories: 505, Fat: 37.7g, Net Carbohydrates: 8.6g, Protein: 25.5g

To Make Low Carb Crust

Ingredients

11/4 cup of ground flax seed

1 small onion

2 tbsp olive oil

¼ ground sunflower seeds

½ apple cider vinegar

1/3 tsp salt

½ tsp baking powder

1 clove garlic, minced, to taste

Directions

1. Preheat oven to 230°F. In a bowl, blend onion with vinegar and oil.

2. Combine the rest of the Ingredients in another bowl and then add onion mixture. Paste should be thick but not crumbly, otherwise add a little water.

3. Place mixture in a greased mold. Form crust with a spoon or with your watered hand. Bake 90 minutes until dry and crunchy.

4. Remove and add filling of choice.

Nutrition Per Serving (per 1/5 crust)

Calories: 294, Fat: 24.8g, Net Carbohydrates: 2.4g, Protein: 8.5g

LUNCH

Hemp Cabbage Salad
Pretty and awesomely healthy.

Servings: 2-3

Preparation time: 10 minutes

Cooking time: 0 minutes

Ingredients:

3 cups of mixed purple and green cabbage, finely shredded

1/4 cup of hemp seeds

1/4 cup of yellow and red peppers chopped

3 tablespoons of hemp oil

3 tablespoons of chopped cilantro

1 1/2 tablespoons of lime juice

1 1/2 avocados, pitted and chopped

Directions:

Mix all the ingredients together in a large bowl.

Nutrition Per Serving

Calories: 381, Fat: 36g, Carbohydrates: 8.7g, Protein: 6.6g

DINNER

Pumpkin Stuffed Mushroom

Low in saturated fat, these protein- rich and gluten-free keto pumpkin stuff mushrooms are a pleasant delight.

Servings: 5

Preparation time: 10 minutes

Cooking time: 30 minutes

Ingredients:

6 portabella mushrooms caps (about 5" in diameter)

1 cup walnuts, chopped

2 tbsp nutritional yeast

1/2 cup canned pumpkin

2 tablespoons of ground flaxseed

1/2 tsp paprika

1/2 tsp salt

1/2 tsp onion powder

1/2 teaspoon of garlic powder

Ground black pepper to taste

Directions:

1. Preheat oven to 350°F

2. Prepare the mushrooms by removing stems and gills and taking out any dirt or debris. Set prepared mushrooms to one side.

3. Now chop the mushroom stems finely and do same to one of the caps.

4. In a medium sized bowl, combine the spices, flaxseed, nutritional yeast and salt. Add the pumpkin into the spice mixture and stir to combine well. Add walnuts and the mushrooms and mix thoroughly until uniform.

5. Divide the filling and share to remaining five mushroom caps.

6. Finally, bake until the caps are shrunken and all is tender, that should take about 30 minutes. Cool a while and enjoy.

Nutrition Per Serving

Calories: 175.2, Fat: 13.6g, Carbohydrates: 6g, Protein: 7.2g

Day 30

BREAKFAST

Tofu Scramble

Servings: 1

Preparation time: minutes

Cooking time: 2-4 minutes

Ingredients:

1 block firm tofu

½ cup cherry tomatoes or peppers

1 tablespoon of olive oil

½ cup frozen spinach

Onion powder, to taste

Garlic powder, to taste

Salt and pepper, to taste

1 pinch turmeric, for color (optional)

Directions:

1. Add all ingredients to a pan. Sauté on medium or low heat for a couple of minutes

2. Serve and enjoy!

LUNCH

Minty Apple & Cabbage Slaw

With your keto-friendly granny smith apples, you can enjoy the taste of this lovely dish.

Servings: 10

Preparation time: 15 minutes

Cooking time: 0 minutes

Ingredients:

8 cups of red cabbage, shredded

2 cups of Granny Smith apples, raw &chopped

1/4 cup of avocado oil

1/4 cup of chopped fresh mint

2 tablespoons of apple cider vinegar

1 tablespoon of lemon juice

1 tablespoon of sugar substitute, granulated

Directions:

1. Toss the chopped apples with the lemon juice to ensure that they do not turn brown.

2. Add to a large salad bowl and mix with the mint and cabbage.

3. In a small bowl, whisk the vinegar, sweetener and oil together.

4. Drizzle the dressing over the salad and toss to coat.

Nutrition Per Serving

Calories: 80, Fat: 6g, Carbohydrates: 5.5g, Protein: 1g

DINNER

Tempeh Stir Fry With Spicy Sauce

Enjoy this easy Asian dinner; it's gluten free and healthy and made with broccoli and mushrooms that is topped with a creamy and spicy sauce.

Servings: 3

Preparation time: 10 minutes

Cooking time: 15 minutes

Ingredients:

8 oz package tempeh, cut into 1" by 2" rectangular strips

3 tablespoons olive oil, divided

8 oz mushrooms, halved & sliced thinly

8 oz broccoli, trimmed of 1 inch ends and cut into 2 inch segments

1 tablespoon ginger, minced

1 tablespoon garlic minced

For The dressing:

1 tablespoon chili garlic sauce

3 tablespoons tahini

2 tablespoons tamari

1 tablespoon maple syrup

1 tablespoon sesame oil

Directions:

1. Add 2 tbsp of oil in a pan and heat over medium high. Add the tempeh and cook until browned per side, remove from pan.

137

2. Add 1 tablespoon of oil and mushrooms, and cook 2- 3 more minutes. Remove.

3. Now add broccoli to the pan as well as ginger and garlic. Let it cook a few minutes and then add the tempeh and mushrooms, mixing well.

4. Combine the sauce ingredients in a bowl and mix well.

5. Serve the tempeh drizzled with sauce. Enjoy, garnished with Sriracha

Nutrition Per Serving

Calories: 481, Fat: 35g, Carbohydrates: 20g, Protein: 22g

SNACK RECIPES

Ready-to-Eat Snacks

Snacking is very important in meal planning. They help to ensure you stay in ketosis and maintain weight loss. There are ready-to-eat snacks that require little or no preparation that you can snack on when you want a quick fix.

To ensure you remain in ketosis, here are some ready –to–eat snack to try:

- Seeds: flax, sunflower, chia and pumpkin. Roasted pumpkin seeds in particular, are high in fat, low in carb and super delicious. It is loaded with zinc that helps to boost the immune system. Sunflower seeds are another snack that's good for you. Chi and flaxseed are high in omega 3s.

- Nuts: Dried coconut is low in carb, high in fats and MCTs. Macadamia nuts are also low in carbs and high in fat and taste great! Pecans and walnuts are low carbs snacks that you can try by spreading equal portions in baking sheet, sprinkled over with cinnamon and toasted lightly. Their oils are good for the skin too. However, some nuts like peanuts, cashews, and pistachios are a little high in carbs.

- Avocados: these are fiber-rich whole foods that are easy to eat. Simply add a little salt and pepper and you are good.

- Seaweed Snacks: salty and high in iodine, this portable and convenient snack is available in range of flavors. However check to see that there aren't added ingredients that'll increase the carbohydrate content.

- Cocoa Nibs: a great alternative to chocolate chips or chocolate bars.

- Coconut Milk Yoghurt: especially the unsweetened vanilla with some stevia sprinkled over and some nuts or hemp seeds on top. Yummy!

- Cherry Tomatoes: quite low in carbs and pair relatively well with basil and olive oil.

- Stevia sweetened Dark chocolate.

- Nut Butters: Peanut, almond, cashew and coconut.

- Veggie Sticks: Slice any vegan keto vegetable and refrigerate. This makes them easy to grab and eat. For instance, a 3-4 inch celery piece that's spread with some hummus or tahinu and sprinkled with sesame seeds on top is a healthy filling snack to try.

- Bars: Quest bars, these low carb but high in protein; therefore eat sparingly. Protein bars are great to try when you are in a rush.

Some popular vegan keto homemade snack alternatives include smoothies, cookies, protein shakes and fat bombs that are loaded with healthy fats and super easy to make. Below are a few homemade snack recipes, complete with nutritional information to add to your meal plans. Bon appétit!

Homemade Vegan Keto Snack Recipes

Cookie Dough Bites

Servings: Yields 30 bites

Serving Size: 3 cookie dough bites

Preparation time: 10 minutes

Cooking time: 0minutes

Ingredients:

1 container (8 oz) vegan cream cheese

3/4 cup almond flour, finely ground

2 tablespoons of sugar free chocolate, chopped

1 teaspoon vanilla extract

1/4 teaspoon liquid stevia, or more, to taste

1/4 tsp almond extract

Directions:

1. Combine the vegan cream cheese extracts and stevia in a bowl; add the almond meal and sugar-free chocolate, and stir thoroughly until fully incorporated.

2. Ladle into silicon muffin tray or muffin liners.

3. Refrigerate for 3-5 hours until solid.

Nutrition Per Serving

Calories: 130, Fat: 12g, Carbohydrates: 2g, Protein: 3g

2-ingredient Keto Fudge

Servings: Yields 3/4 cup of fudge

Serving Size: 1/8th of recipe

Preparation time: 15minutes

Cooking time: 10 minutes

Ingredients:

2 oz sugar- free chocolate or 2 ounces bakers chocolate & 15 drops liquid stevia

1/2 cup nut butter such as coconut butter

Directions:

1. Begin by lining the container with wax paper (for coconut butter users).

2. Melt the chocolate and coconut butter together and continuously stir so it doesn't burn and to ensure the ingredients are well incorporated.

3. Pour the mixture into the lined container and place in the refrigerator for 30 to 45 minutes until hard.

4. Take out and cut into pieces.

Nutrition Per Serving

Calories: 123, Fat: 10.9g, Carbohydrates: 1.4g, Protein: 1.5g

White Chocolate Peanut Butter Bites

Servings: Yields 24 pieces

Serving Size: 1 piece

Preparation time: 75minutes

Cooking time: 0minutes

Ingredients:

1/2 cup peanut butter (salted)

1/2 cup cacao butter

3 tbsp swerve

4 tbsp powdered coconut milk or 1 scoop of unflavored whey powder

1/4 tsp vanilla extract

Directions:

1. Melt the cacao butter and peanut butter together. Add the vanilla extract and stir well.

2. Combine the whey and swerve in a separate bowl.

3. Now add in the swerve mixture, a tablespoon at a time, mixing to incorporate well before adding in the next tablespoon.

4. Transfer to mold or lined muffin tin; refrigerate 60 to 90 minutes to set well, remove from tray and enjoy.

Nutrition Per Serving

Calories: 77, Fat: 7.3g, Carbohydrates: .8g, Protein: 2.2g

Lavender Blueberry Fat Bombs

Sugar free and nut-free

Servings: Yields 10 fat bombs

Serving Size: 1 fat bomb

Preparation time: 15minutes

Cooking time: 0minutes

Ingredients:

3/4 cup coconut oil

1/2 cup hemp hearts

1 tsp beetroot powder

1/4 tsp culinary lavender

1/4 cup of blueberries

1 tsp vanilla extract

10-15 drops of liquid stevia

Pinch of salt

Directions:

1. In a blender or processor, add in all the ingredients (except the blueberries) and blend until smooth or for a minute to ensure the hemp hearts blend well.

2. Now add the blueberries and pulse again until chopped but not blended fully.

3. Pour equal portions into muffin pans or silicon trays. Refrigerate until solid.

Nutrition Per Serving

Calories: 192, Fat: 19.1g, Carbohydrates: .7g, Protein: 2g

Cucumber Green Smoothie

Servings: 1

Preparation time: 2 minutes

Cooking time: minutes

Ingredients:

2 handfuls spinach

21/2 ounces cucumber, peeled & cubed

7 large ice cubes

1-2 tablespoon MCT Oil

1 cup coconut milk

¼ teaspoon xanthan gum

12 drops liquid Stevia

Directions:

1. Combine all the ingredients in a blender and blend to desired consistency.

2. Pour out and enjoy!

Nutrition Per Serving

Calories: 330, Fat: 32.34 g, Carbohydrates: 2.91g, Protein: 10.14g

Strawberry Milkshake

Servings: 1

Preparation time: 2 minutes

Cooking time: 0minutes

Ingredients:

3/4 cup coconut milk

1/4 cup coconut cream

7 ice cubes

2 tbsp. strawberry torani, sugar-free

1 tablespoon of MCT oil

1/4 teaspoon xanthan gum

Directions:

1. Combine all the ingredients in a blender and blend to desired consistency.

2. Pour out and enjoy!

Nutrition Per Serving

Calories: 368, Fat: 38.85 g, Carbohydrates: 2.42g, Protein: 1.69g

Cucumber Dill Hummus

Servings: Yields 3 cups hummus

Preparation time: 2 minutes

Cooking time: 0minutes

Ingredients:

2 cups cubed cucumber

1 can (1.75 cups) chickpeas

1/4 cup tahini

5 cloves roasted garlic

1/4 cup apple cider vinegar

1 teaspoon dried dill

1/2 teaspoon salt

Directions:

1. Add all ingredients to a blender and pulse until smooth

Nutrition Per Serving

Calories: 36, Fat: 1.9 g, Carbohydrates: 2.8g, Protein: 1.1g

Brown Protein Balls

Get the energy for your workouts and all through the day.

Servings: Yields 30 protein balls

Servings: 10

Preparation time: 15 minutes

Cooking time: 0minutes

Ingredients:

1 cup almond butter or peanut butter

3 scoops of vegan protein powder

1 cup unsweetened dried coconut

1/4 cup ground flax seed

1 tsp vanilla extract

Directions:

1. Add together in a bowl and mix thoroughly.

2. Refrigerate for 30- 60 minutes to enable the mixture form balls.

3. Mold into little balls (30 in number) and refrigerate for up to a week.

Nutrition Per Serving

Calories: 259, Fat: 20.9 g, Carbohydrates: 3.6g, Protein: 12.4g

Coco Butter Cups

Servings: Yields 30 protein balls

Servings: 4

Preparation time: 20 minutes

Cooking time: 0minutes

Ingredients:

4 tablespoons of cocoa powder

2 tablespoons of erythritol

4 tablespoons of coconut oil

4 teaspoons coconut butter

1 pinch salt

Directions:

1. Combine cocoa powder, coconut oil, and erythritol in a bowl and stir until clump-free. Add salt for sweetness.

2. Pour half of the chocolate mixture into silicone cupcake molds evenly on a plate and freeze for about 5 minutes.

3. Once the bottom layer is hard, spoon1 teaspoon of coconut butter each onto the molds and freeze for 2-3 minutes.

4. Covered the hardened butter with the chocolate mixture that's left. Freeze again for 5 more minutes. Enjoy!

Nutrition Per Serving

Calories: 260, Fat: 27g, Carbohydrates: 0.5g, Protein: 3g

Salted Almond And Coconut

Servings: 12 fat bombs

Preparation time: 25minutes

Cooking time: 10minutes

Ingredients:

1/2 cup almonds

1/2 cup unsweetened flaked coconut

3.5ounce dark chocolate

1/2 cup coconut butter

1/2 tsp almond extract (optional)

10 drops liquid stevia (optional)

1/4 tsp sea salt

Directions:

1. Preheat the oven to 350°F.

2. Combine the almonds and coconut and spread onto a foil-lined baking sheet. Toast in the oven for 5 to 8 minutes, stirring infrequently so it doesn't burn. Set aside baking sheet to cool.

2. Melt the dark chocolate in a double boiler and add to the coconut butter, stirring well. Add the almond extract and liquid stevia, if using). Mix and set to one side.

3. Pour chocolate mixture in a lined baking sheet 9 with parchment paper) and spread evenly with the back of spoon.

4. Sprinkle the toasted almond as well as the coconut flakes over it and press down gently with hands to ensure the ingredients touch the chocolate. Sprinkle sea salt and chill for 1 to 2 hours to set.

5. Afterwards, slice and enjoy

Nutrition Per Serving

Calories: 173, Fat: 16g, Carbohydrates: 3.5g, Protein: 3g

Keto Protein Shake

Servings: 1

Preparation time: 5minutes

Cooking time: 0minutes

Ingredients:

1 tablespoon cocoa powder

1 cup almond milk

1 tablespoon peanut butter

1 tablespoon coconut oil

2 teaspoons erythritol

1 scoop chocolate protein powder

4 ice cubes

Directions:

1. Add all the ingredients together in a blender or processor.

2. Blend and enjoy cold

Nutrition Per Serving

Calories: 385, Fat: 26g, Carbohydrates: 4.5g, Protein: 30g

Mediterranean Flat Bread

Servings: 1 flatbread

Preparation time: 5minutes

Cooking time: minutes

Ingredients:

For The Flat Bread:

6 crispbread pieces (check table of content for recipe)

For The Topping

1/4 cup sundried tomatoes

1/2 cup kitted kalamata olives

2 stalks of green onions

1/4 cup fresh parsley

1 tsp lemon juice

1/4 cup fresh dill

1 tbsp olive oil

Pepper, to taste

Directions:

1. Make the flatbread.

2. While it is cooking, chop up the tomatoes, olives, parsley scallions and dill and place in a bowl.

3. Add lemon juice, pepper, and olive oil to the tomato/ olive mixture and toss until well mixed. Chill mixture while the flatbread continues to cook.

5. Once flatbread is cooked, remove from oven, cool and spread 1 teapoon of hummus on each of them. Drizzle olive mixture evenly on top of and enjoy.

Nutrition Per Serving

Calories: 221, Fat: 18.1g, Carbohydrates: 4.8g, Protein: 6.6g

White Chocolate Raspberry Cups

Servings: 12 raspberry cups

Preparation time: 10minutes

Cooking time: 5minutes

Ingredients:

1/2 cup cacao butter

1/2 cup coconut manna

4 tbsp powdered coconut milk

 tbsp granulated sugar substitute such as swerve

1 tsp vanilla extract

1/4 cup freeze dried raspberries, crushed

Directions:

1. In a double boiler, melt cacao butter and coconut manna until thoroughly mixed. Add vanilla extract and stir.

2. In a separate dish, mix coconut milk powder and swerve together.

3. Add the coconut milk powder / swerve mixture into the cacao butter a tablespoon at a time to ensure it is fully incorporated before adding in the next spoon.

4. Mix the raspberries in and divide to muffin tins

5. Refrigerate an hour to set.

Nutrition Per Serving

Calories: 158, Fat: 15.5g, Carbohydrates: g, Protein: 2.6g

The End

Made in the USA
Middletown, DE
02 July 2018